THE SPIRIT OF MERCY
ON THE WEST TEXAS WIND

A history of the Monastery of the Most Pure Heart of Mary
and Our Lady of Mercy Academy and Convent
Stanton, Martin County, Texas

Rosa Walston Latimer
For Martin County Convent Foundation, Inc.

Copyright © 2021 Martin County Convent Foundation, Inc.

All rights reserved. This book or any portion thereof may not be reproduced or used in any manner whatsoever without the express written permission of the publisher except for the use of brief quotation in a book review.

First printing, 2021.

ISBN: 978-0-578-96134-7

Martin County Convent Foundation, Inc.
P.O. Box 1435
Stanton, Texas, 79782

www.hcmstanton.org

Their bodies have been buried in peace,
and their names live on for all generations.
The people will proclaim their wisdom,
the assembly will celebrate their praises.
- Anonymous

CONTENTS

Foreword 1
Introduction 5

   1. The Railroad Makes a Path for Religion 11
   2. A Renegade Priest and a Band of Brothers 16
   3. Grelton Emerges as Thriving Marienfeld....................22
   4. Carmelite Commitment and Courage 32
   5. Nature Does Not Make Her a Paradise 40
   6. Death at the Monastery 48
   7. Schooling Comes to the Staked Plains 51
   8. A Thorough and Refined Education 54
   9. Accredited Edification and Enrichment 65
   10. A Look Back at Learning 77
   11. The Academy in Ruins 95
   12. An Enduring Heritage 105

Appendix I –
The Sisters of Our Lady of Mercy..109

Appendix II -
Articles of Corporation Sisters of Mercy Educational Society...113

Appendix III -
Sisters of Mercy Educational Society of Texas By-Laws............115

Acknowledgments 117
Selected Bibliography 119
About the Author 121
Index...123

Foreword

I remember the day I first had the opportunity to walk through the Carmelite Monastery in Stanton, Texas. I was a teacher in a small school north of Stanton and have always been interested in history and, in particular, Texas history. The county extension agent led me through the ornate Victorian iron gate on the south end of the property that leads to the historic monastery building. The building was covered in red railroad beadboard and the wonderful Gothic pointed windows were boarded uptight. Inside, the rooms were illuminated by bare bulbs from much earlier two-stranded electrical wiring. The room smelled of the all too familiar West Texas dust, which covered every surface. I could not believe my good fortune to be in an unrestored building from 1884 made of four-foot-thick adobe brick walls with Gothic windows. Walking inside was like being transported to another time and era of the isolated West Texas settlements along the Texas and Pacific Railway. A time when few barely passable roads existed and the railroads were the only way to move goods and people when individuals and groups were looking to escape the crowded cities and headed to a very different landscape and climate; looking for a chance to begin a new life on the High Plains with the opportunity to buy cheap land offered by the railroads and create close-knit communities based on liked interests, ethnicities, and ideals.

Walking through this building with 100 plus years of history cannot be underestimated. It provides a look back in time that a museum display could never fully convey. It has been described by the late architect and adobe expert Paul G. McHenry as one of the finest historic adobe structures in the American Southwest. This was the feeling as I walked through the small doors into rooms with squeaky floorboards and peeling paint. I was enchanted from the very beginning by the building and the story of the monks that built it with adobe laborers from Ysleta and of the sisters who gave tirelessly to teach young girls and boys from Stanton and elsewhere on the wide-open prairie. These included children living on ranches with little chance for formal education if it were not for this place in Stanton, halfway between Fort Worth and El Paso.

Our Lady of Mercy Academy and Convent main building before restoration. Photo date unknown. *Martin County Foundation, Inc.*

The history and settlement of Stanton and the West Texas area are tied closely with this monastery. Its restoration is the result of countless hours of hard work by volunteers who believe it is important to preserve

Martin County Convent Foundation

history. I hope you enjoy reading this account of the Historic Carmelite Monastery and Our Lady of Mercy Academy and that it encourages you to pay a visit.

John Kennady
Historian and member of Martin County Convent Foundation, Inc.

Introduction

In 1881, a settlement, originally called Grelton, approximately 325 miles east of El Paso, Texas, sprang to life among mesquite and scrub oak trees. The tiny outpost existed solely to serve a new railroad line as a watering terminal. A year later, Grelton was given a new name and elevated to a higher calling.

The potential for Grelton as a religious, educational, and agricultural center came together in the vision of Father Anastasius Peters O.Carm. The German priest saw Grelton and the surrounding area as "Mary's Field," or "Marienfeld," to honor the Virgin Mary. The new, melodic-sounding name for the remote settlement also elicited visions of verdant fields and prosperity, although even on a clear spring morning, one could see gathering dust on the horizon.

Father Peters saw the opportunity for an unbroken circle in Marienfeld. The development of the outpost as a farming community would attract families with children. Those families would support a Catholic school and monastery and also establish ongoing financial support for St. Joseph parish. In turn, this financial foundation would sanction the travel of priests throughout the remote mission field of West Texas, providing the opportunity to fulfill a loyalty to their ministry. A good plan. Perhaps, with providential blessing, Father Peters' vision would become a reality.

Indeed, families and businesses came to Marienfeld. In four years, a church, a two-story monastery, and many homes were built. A school was established. Young men came to receive training for the priesthood.

A special correspondent for *The Galveston County Daily News* wrote in October of 1884 that Marienfeld was at that time "one of the most interesting spots in Texas to me. Wherever I have wandered, my thoughts have often gone back to Marienfeld because it involved an experiment which, if successful, would prove that vast region of Texas known as the Staked Plains to be one of the most desirable parts of the state." In December 1884, Martin County was established with Marienfeld as the county seat.

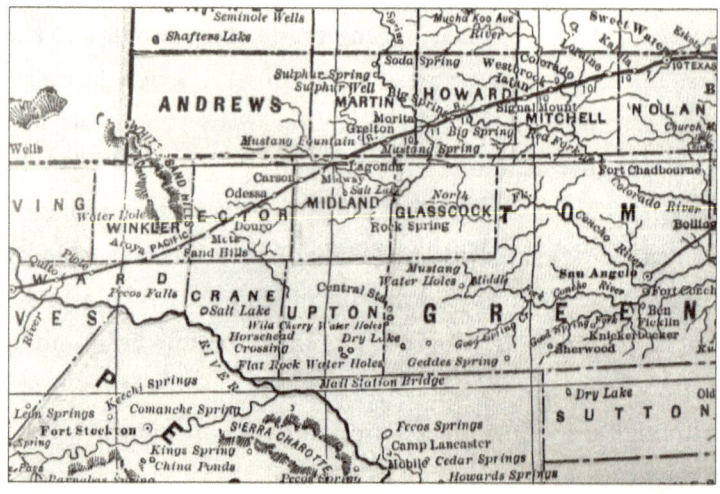

Map published ca. 1884 of Martin County area of Texas. *John Kennady.*

A year later, Father Anastasius traveled to Dallas, Texas, to promote the potential of Marienfeld and sell lots in the developing community. *The Dallas Morning News* published a lengthy interview with the priest in which he touted the "agricultural prosperity with much potential for growth, lack of crime and a fine Catholic school." However, the success of Mary's Field would be short-lived.

In a letter to a family member, an early Marienfeld settler, Mrs. W.F. Fahrenkempt, described the downturn of events during the next eighteen months.

"In 1885, the grass was plentiful, being almost knee-high, while wheat and cotton were fine. In 1886 the drought began. What before had been green fields of wheat was now burned, and withered stubble and sandstorms reigned supreme."

Crops failed. Many settlers returned to their previous homes. Some moved 20 miles northeast to Big Spring to work for the Texas and Pacific Railway, while others took jobs with ranches in the area.

The intense drought continued until 1888, with severe winter storms adding peril in 1887 and 1888. The loss of so many Catholic farming families at Marienfeld produced a new Protestant majority, and in 1890, a local referendum changed the name of the town to Stanton. The next few years saw the organization of several Protestant congregations.

After the devastating drought, other than St. Joseph Catholic Church, all that remained of Father Anastasius' original vision for the settlement was the Catholic school. The symbol of that school is still with us — a stately two-story adobe building on a slight hill overlooking the town.

The Carmelite priests struggled to maintain their ministry in the far-spread mission field of West Texas. Father Anastasius enlisted Sisters of Divine Providence nuns to continue the parochial school for young boys and girls; however, by 1891, the school had closed.

The possibility of maintaining a parochial school in this remote community appeared impossible. However, a conversation in the train depot of El Paso, Texas, between a nun traveling back home to San Francisco after visiting family in the East and a German Carmelite priest renewed hope. In 1894, with a decisive purpose and commitment to serve,

Sister Mary Berchmans Kast and a small group of Sisters of Mercy nuns reopened the Stanton school with 16 pupils. Our Lady of Mercy Academy and Convent would educate thousands of local boys and girls and students from across the United States for the next 44 years.

(l to r) Cecilia, John, Alma, Joe, and Dorothy Herzog, children of Henry and Annie (Stoeger) Herzog. The family lived in Stanton and the children walked to Our Lady of Mercy Academy to attend school. *Georgeann Walton.*

The contribution of the 19th-century German settlement to the development of this remote area of Texas was powerful. The establishment of a religious and educational center when Martin County was largely uncivilized was notably optimistic. However, perhaps the most consequential, far-reaching impact of the Monastery of the Most Pure Heart of Mary and Our Lady of Mercy Academy and Convent is the humanity and altruism shown by those who served there. Our intention in publishing this book is to give an overview of the monastery, academy, and convent history. Also, to pay homage to the individuals who were instrumental in the founding of the religious community, maintaining an educational center, and the students who studied there.

Preservation of the surviving adobe monastery building that served as the heart of the convent compound is significant. The structure provides a lasting, tangible repository for the memories of those who worked, learned, and worshipped there. This remains holy ground and recalls for us the dignity and determination that created a lasting foundation of values that continues to influence life in Martin County today.

As you can imagine, over the course of almost 150 years, historical details are not always consistent. From the wealth of research material available for the writing of this book, there were a few discrepancies in the telling of stories. When we encountered this, we deferred to the research and writing of Fr. John-Benedict Weber, O.Carm. and information obtained for the archives of Mercy Heritage Center, Sisters of Mercy of the Americas, and the Catholic Archives of Texas.

Chapter 1
The Railroad Makes a Path for Religion

The outlying Staked Plains of Texas were mostly undeveloped until 1881 when the Texas and Pacific Railway laid tracks from Fort Worth to Sierra Blanca, Texas, the completion point of a southern transcontinental railway. Grelton, almost the mid-point of this stretch of tracks, was one of many section stations established by the "T & P" approximately every ten miles.

Before the railroad cut through this distant part of Texas, there was no civilization on these plains except Native Americans who traveled through the area. Buffalo, antelope, and other wild game were plentiful. Tribes of Lipan Apaches originally dominated the Staked Plains region but were later displaced by the Comanches. Capt. John Pope, a topographical engineer, saw Native Americans in the area when he scouted in 1854. A spring-fed lake, later known as Mustang Springs or Pond, was a frequent campsite.

According to a report by Terry Jordan, Professor of Geography at North Texas State University, as early as 1850, persons of German birth or descent formed the largest ethnic group in Texas derived directly from Europe. Thirty years before the founding of Grelton, German-born settlers made up over five percent of the total Texas population (approximately 20,000). However, most of these immigrants settled in enclaves in south-central Texas.

In the 1983 *Panhandle-Plains Historical Review*, Don Abbe described the process by which this vast, remote part of the great state of Texas was settled.

> "The expansion of the railroad provided both the stimulus and the means needed to initiate settlement along its route. The Texas and Pacific established a land office in Marshall, Texas, to facilitate land sales. The railroad platted towns all along its new right-of-way and launched a massive campaign to sell over five million acres of Texas land, including 200,832 Martin County acres."

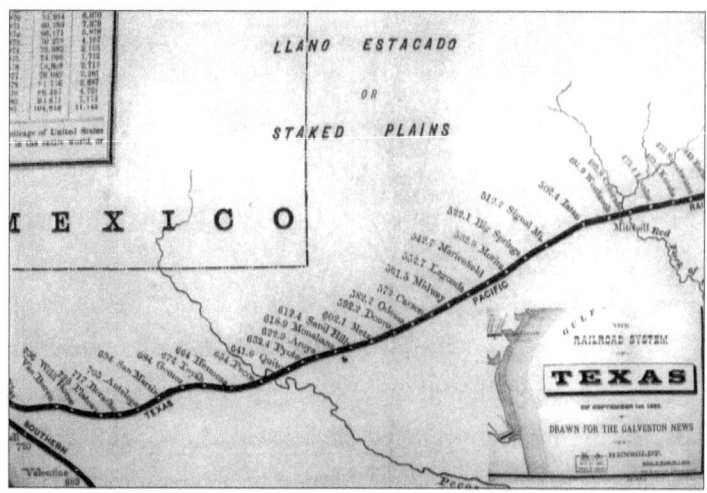

The railroad system of Texas in 1883. Drawn by E.A. Hensoldt for the *Galveston News. Library of Congress.*

The price for this open land started at one dollar per acre. Lots in the newly formed towns sold for twenty-five dollars each. Immigrants were targeted by railroad advertising, and hundreds were attracted to this once-isolated part of the state. This opportunity to own land was especially attractive to German immigrants, many of whom left their home country seeking better economic conditions and religious freedom.

Early history reports a meeting early in 1882, a year after the railroad created the Grelton settlement, between John Jacob Konz, a German immigrant living in Kansas, and W. H. Abrams, a land agent for the Texas and Pacific Railway. Mr. Konz was looking for a location for a German colony in Texas. Mr. Abrams described "rich, unoccupied and untilled lands that lay along the railway line." This vast, remote area appealed to Mr. Konz, and he set plans in motion to resettle in Grelton. John Konz and his wife, Mary, are thought to be the first settlers at Grelton who were not attached to the Carmelite community.

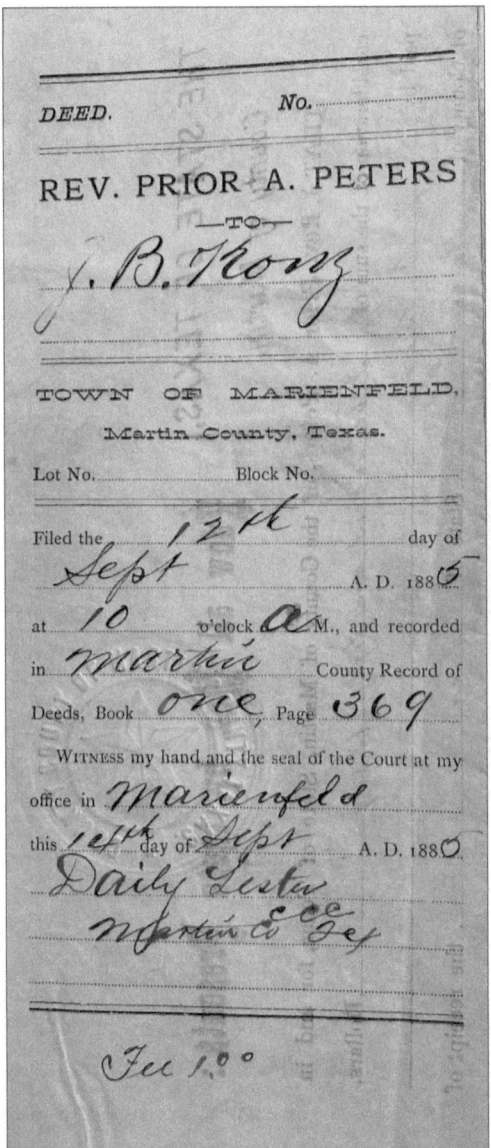

1885 deed from Father Anastasius Peters to J.B. Konz for land in Martin County, Texas. *Georgeann Walton.*

Two brothers, Christian and Leonard Peters, born in Breberen, Germany, to a devoted, religious family, would be what might seem the unlikely driving force behind the establishment of a religious and educational center in West Texas.

The founder of the Martin County parish and monastery, Christian Dominikus Peters, born October 5, 1844, was the sixth of nine children born to Godfried and Sophia Peters. According to a biography in the publication *Der Peters Familie* by Ernestine Peters Schmidt, when Christian was a young man, he attended college at Kempen, Germany, to become a teacher. While at college, he fell in love with a young lady, and the couple

Texas & Pacific Railway Deed for 160 acres of land 1 ½ miles northwest of Ma-rienfeld, Texas. *Georgeann Walton.*

planned to marry. "However, his fiancée died before they could be married. Shortly afterward, Christian decided to join his younger brother in Holland to study to become a priest." Christian entered the monastery in 1868 and began his novice a year later. "In September 1876, almost 32 years old and eight years after having entered the Carmelite Order, Christian Dominikus was ordained a priest. At this time, according to custom, his name was changed, and he became known as Father Anastasius Peters." Within a few years, Fr. Anastasius went to the United States to serve at the St. Boniface Monastery in Scipio, Kansas.

Leonard Peters was four years younger than his brother and entered the Order of the Carmelites in 1866. Leonard was ordained to the priesthood in 1872 and accepted the name Father Boniface Peters. The priest transferred to Scipio, Kansas, in 1880, where he served as master of novices.

A third Peters brother, Peter Peters, born in 1850, joined the Order of the Carmelites at the age of 17. He was ordained to the priesthood in 1873, assuming the name of Father Hubertus. According to the Peters family history, he served in Germany until 1877 when he emigrated to North America and entered the Holy Trinity Monastery in Pittsburgh, Pennsylvania. "Later, he left the Carmelites and entered the Capuchin Province of St. Augustine, where he made profession in 1883, taking the name of Padre Herman Joseph." This Peters brother was not part of the founding and development of the Monastery of the Most Pure Heart of Mary in Texas. The youngest child born to the Godfried Peters family was a daughter, Theresa, who entered the convent at the age of 16 and became a Carmelite nun known only as Sister Theresa. She served 43 years in a Carmelite Cloister in Belgium, where she died in March of 1911.

Chapter 2
A Renegade Priest and a Band of Brothers

In early August of 1882, after leaving the St. Boniface Monastery in Scipio, Kansas, Carmelite priests Father Boniface Peters and Father Anthony Keber joined Fr. Boniface's brother, Father Anastasius, and Adam Konz at Grelton Station. Three novices also came to Texas from the Kansas monastery: Albert Wagner, Berthold Ohlenforst, and Andrew Fuhrwerk. Three years later, these novices were the first Carmelites ordained to the priesthood in Texas.

While we may not determine the exact circumstances surrounding the break with St. Boniface Monastery in Kansas by these brothers, we know the separation was not amicable.

Correspondence archives indicate that in June 1882, the provincial superior at St. Boniface, Father Smits, dismissed Father Anastasius Peters from his responsibilities as prior and pastor at the Kansas monastery. Father Smits, known to be a pious and rigid man, took this severe action because of what he viewed as Father Anastasius' open revolt against a directive from the Prior General of the Carmelites in Rome. The directive called for the unification of all of the American and Canadian monasteries of the

Order. Correspondence between Father Smits and Bishop John C. Neraz of the San Antonio, Texas Diocese provides a more thorough description of the probable reason Father Anastasius Peters and the small group of Carmelites made their way to Texas.

Carmelite priests of the Monastery of the Most Pure Heart of Mary ca. 1890. Front row, beginning second from left: Fr. Albert Wagner, Fr. Anastasius Peters, Fr. Boniface Peters, Fr. Simon Weeg. *John-Benedict Weber, O.Carm.*

In his handwritten, five-page letter to the Bishop, Father Smits refers to Father Anastasius Peters as a renegade and offers his candid opinion of the Carmelite priests who began the Catholic mission at Grelton, within the San Antonio Diocese:

> "I consider it my conscientious duty to give you some further information about this Rev. Anast. Peters & party. I would not do it if they did not intend settling down in your diocese; for you ought to know with what kind of people you will have to deal… since I desire only to check evil, and not to hurt any one [sic], more than justice demands, or rather the good of religion."

Father Smits also states in his letter that Father Boniface Peters and the friars accompanying his departure from the Kansas monastery left secretly in the early morning of August 6, 1882. He accuses them of taking three trunks containing household goods and farm implements from the monastery as well as one thousand dollars in cash.

> "He [Fr. Boniface Peters] had an opportunity to take all of these things because he was acting local superior up to the moment he left. The money was in his hands, and the goods were collected without the knowledge of the new superior, and all others did not know, but that it was to be so…The fathers Peters are 3 brothers in the Order, and were received into it in the Province of Holland. Their names in religion (according to age) are Anastasius, Boniface, and Hubert Peters. They are Prussians."

The letter continues to describe what Father Smits considers to be a history of the questionable character of the Peters brothers and their negative influence on the reputation of Carmelites in Kansas:

> "They did very well before they were priests, but after that, almost immediately became restless and discontented through Anastasius. They ran away from the monastery…and fell into the same censures, as this time, apparently, so their own superior told me when I was in Europe in 1876. The Sup. General at Rome in his kindness pardoned them at their showing repentance, and transferred them to Bavaria. They got into trouble in Bavaria, I do not know how, or whereby; I was told they had even to appear before court. Thereupon they were sent to America. At that time, the Carmelites were very few and scattered here and there to address mission churches.
>
> "Fr. Aust. Peters, far away from all observers [in Kansas] carried on in high style, received all kinds of people. He took in

numbers of suspended priests, seculars, and other religions without regard to the provisions of the Rule. Oh! he ruined us in Kansas. Our name became almost a byword there...It was a terrible cross to us. I do not know how he can very well and safely be trusted alone on a mission. His brothers are very moral men, and have made good studies. Anastasius has the reputation for ignorance and great daring and impertinence. He leads the other two, and they go with him, as children follow their parents."

In this lengthy personal letter, Father Smits further attributes a disruptive attitude to the Peters brothers and warns the Bishop not to allow them to work in his diocese in Texas. He even suggests that the brothers leave the Carmelite Order altogether. Fr. Smits provided the names of others to verify his information regarding Father Anastasius Peters, "in case Your Rt. Reverence thinks that I say too much."

"[The Peters brothers] would rather have the Germans alone, and refused to live with other nationalities...Fr. Hubert Peters is a good man, but of course, as discontented as his brothers, he is afraid of other nationalities. He wishes, if he can, to enter a German Religious house, otherwise be secularized. It would be the greatest Blessings if these poor Fathers were to leave us. Under no circumstances allow them to start any other religious Order in your diocese, as they are not fit subjects for it.

"Now, Rt. Rev. & dear Bishop, I regret very much to have taken up so much of your valuable time, and probably annoyed you with so long a story, but I was most desirous to do so in order that not through my negligence your Rt. Reverence might have any difficulties. Since by knowing them, you will have it easier to treat with them. Again, begging pardon for my intrusion, and asking your episcopal Blessing, I remain with best wishes and highest esteem. Your humble servant in Christ, Anastasius J. Smits, O.C.C."

Father Smits was considered a very stern, staunch Carmelite priest with unquestionable loyalty to the Church. Upon his death in 1938, his obituary described the priest as "one of the most interesting characters in the life of our [Carmelite] Province. His was a unique personality, with unique gifts, unique virtues and, it may be said, with unique faults." Given this insight, it is easy to understand that, what was perceived to be the cavalier personality of Father Anastasius Peters, founder of the Carmelite monastery in Martin County, could easily be at odds with the expectations of his former provincial superior.

Historian John Hutto described Father Anastasius Peters at the time he arrived in Texas as "a man of great energy and foresight."

Respected Carmelite historian and author, Father Joachim Smet, O. C., described Father Anastasius Peters as a man "ahead of his time in his dedication to the need of the moment and disregard for proper procedure...he was a man of...undisciplined energies." Perhaps such a dedicated, dynamic priest was needed to serve those who lived in the isolated Staked Plains of West Texas.

According to research conducted by Carmelite historian Father John-Benedict Weber, the united Carmelite monasteries in the northern United States did not approve of or support the monastery and parish that developed in the Grelton settlement. This withholding of sanction was because the Peters brothers had moved to Texas without prior permission from the Carmelite superiors in Rome and the United States.

Bishop Neraz of San Antonio did not heed the warnings in Father Smits' lengthy letter, nor did he consider these previous actions of the Peters brothers a hindrance to the possibility of their mission in Texas. Instead, the Bishop supported Father Anastasius Peters and what became the Monastery of the Most Pure Heart of Mary by writing testimonial letters to the prior general in Rome. With this action, the Bishop successfully established the independence of the monastery from other Carmelite monasteries in North America. Most likely, at this time in 1882, the Bishop of San Antonio was badly in need of clergymen to minister to the fast-growing immigrant population in West Texas. Possessing a desire to live and work among fellow Germans, Fr. Anastasius and the other priests who accompanied him to Texas seemed especially suited to establish a German Catholic community in this remote part of the state.

Beginning with the arrival of these Carmelites in Texas and continuing with their ministry throughout West Texas, there are no reports of any improprieties. There exists, however, extensive documentation and evidence of an energetic Carmelite ministry working in tough circumstances with little financial stability.

Chapter 3
Grelton Emerges as Thriving Marienfeld

When Father Anastasius Peters and the priests who accompanied him to Texas arrived at Grelton in 1882, most likely all they found was a two-story railroad section house, a pump, and a water tank. The Carmelite priests pitched two tents at the site where the present-day Martin County courthouse sits. One tent was their living quarters, and the other was a place of worship. Father Anastasius Peters petitioned the Texas and Pacific Railway to change the name of the settlement from Grelton to Marienfeld, German for "Mary's Field," and devoted his energies to establishing a religious center and attracting families to the settlement.

Despite the many obstacles in this isolated region of the state, in the three years between 1882 and 1885, the railroad section settlement developed into a thriving community. The priests built a proper adobe structure to house St. Joseph Church. They established a Carmelite religious institution that would serve as a monastery, a church, a parochial school, and a theological seminary. Many families had established new homes in Marienfeld.

Father Telesphorus Hardt, O. C wrote a narrative, "Remembrances and Events from My Life," recounting his time at the Marienfeld monastery during the early years. "Prairie grass then was 2 to 3 meters tall. Rabbits, prairie dogs, tarantulas, scorpions, centipedes, and rattlesnakes abounded. Songbirds and birds of prey – eagles, hawks, and vultures – were common." In his description of the work on the new adobe church, Father Telesphorus mentioned the four-foot-thick walls as well as the double row of bricks laid on the exterior of the church after the adobe had firmly dried "to withstand the fierce West Texas wind." He also told of his labor in laying wooden shingles on the new church and construction accidents involving the bell tower and the front wall of the church. "The local settlers didn't have any money so all the work in building…had to be done by the men of the town working together with Carmelites. Some days we worked as brick-makers. Some days we were brick-layers. Other times, we were carpenters and blacksmiths."

St. Joseph's Church on monastery grounds, C. 1945. *Martin County Foundation, In.*

Many of the newcomers to Marienfeld were relatives of Father Anastasius. After coming to the new mission in Texas, the priest made several trips to Arkansas to visit family, perhaps, in part, to recruit new parishioners for the settlement. During Father Anastasius' absence, his brother, Father Boniface, provided pastoral care for the new parish and monastery community. In that year, the priests purchased over 2500 acres of land from the Texas and Pacific Railroad for twenty-five cents an acre under the auspices of the Settler Act of 1883 enacted by the state legislature. In turn, the priests sold approximately half of the acreage to pay the building costs of the new Carmelite religious center.

Among the early settlers were Father Anastasius' cousins, Johann Jacobs Peters and Frederick Peters and their families, and Nicholas Mundloch and family. Originally from Germany, these families came to America and first settled in Pocahontas, Arkansas, on land purchased through a land agent in Germany. The tree-covered acreage in Arkansas was not a favorable landscape for the Germans to re-establish their farms. The prospects in Martin County, Texas, with its abundant potential for farmland and burgeoning German Catholic community, were reason enough for the families to move west.

Joseph Stoeger, one of the first Marienfeld residents. *Georgeann Walton.*

An article in an April 1883 edition of *The Galveston County Daily News* reported that the community of Marienfeld "boasted over a dozen residences, with numerous more under construction, a Catholic church, a general store, and the railroad depot and water tank. The community contains approximately 100 to 150 people, and is surrounded by farm after farm occupied by German families." The article stressed two major themes of the colony's existence: agriculture and religion. It is likely the report was submitted to the Galveston newspaper by Father Anastasius to attract settlers to Marienfeld.

The Peters family history describes Fr. Anastasius as "a promoter of civic affairs." He organized the settlers in Marienfeld into a society called the German Catholics of the Carmelite Association, and this group contracted with the Texas and Pacific to purchase land. The priest also solicited money from Germany and tried to attract more German settlers. Financial support from Germany became a staple of Carmelite existence during the first decade in West Texas. Many new candidates for the priesthood came from Germany to Marienfeld to begin their formation as Carmelites.

A son, Joseph, was born to Nicholas and Margaretha Mundloch on October 7, 1883, and Peters family history claims him as the "first white child" born in Martin County. His father, Nicholas, died October 31, the same year, and was the first person buried in St. Joseph Cemetery at Marienfeld. Two years later, Nicholas' widow, age 29, married Johann Jacob Peters, age 46, a widower with five children. Theirs was the first marriage license issued in Martin County. "To this union was born eight children."

The extensive Peters family history, *Der Peters Familie*, provides insight into the life and resourcefulness of Jacob and Margaretha Peters:

> "Johann Jacob Peters accumulated almost twelve sections of land north of Marienfeld. At first, he raised sheep, and at one time had about 2,000 head. Jacob shipped wool to several northern cities, including Fort Wayne, Indiana. He also grew vegetables and was

especially successful in raising cabbage and onions, which he sold in the area. Later, Jacob raised cattle, increasing his herd to as high as 600 head. He also grew one of the first cotton crops in Martin County.

"Margaretha was said to have driven a wagon and team to market their produce, and sometimes walked to Big Spring where she sold her butter and eggs. Margaretha also nursed and served as a midwife. She went as far as Big Spring and Colorado City in order to perform her nursing duties. This pioneer woman carried water in a bucket from the town well before water was found on their farm."

The family history also describes the wholesale groceries the Peters family ordered from George Bundy of St. Louis, Missouri. Coffee, sugar, English peas, red beans, and dried fruit arrived on the train in 100-pound sacks.

Trackside stock pens held herds driven by area ranchers to the railhead at Marienfeld waiting for the next train. If the pens were full, ranchers would pay Jacob to keep the overflow in his pasture.

The railroad and Father Anastasius shared the goal of proving that Marienfeld was an attractive place to settle. Fr. Anastasius and his brother, Fr. Boniface, wrote promotional bulletins and even traveled to Germany to publicize the colony. At Marienfeld, sample crops were grown on a demonstration plat. In a narrative published in the October 1933 *West Texas Historical Association Yearbook*, John Hutto described the plat as covering 20 acres located just south of the water tower. Crops included wheat, barley, rye, and oats. "The seasons were good, the yield plentiful."

This bit of success was apparently surprising as an article in the *Galveston County Daily News*, in September 1883, states that "in regard to farming operations on the Staked Plains and to a new German settlement called Marienfeld, in Martin County…the ground had been plowed, the grain was growing, but had not yet matured. It had always been the opinion of those most interested in other pursuits than farming, that crops could not be raised there. The German settlers were met on all sides with doleful predictions of complete failure. Contrary to the expectation of all but the farmers themselves, the results obtained have been highly satisfactory." The article describes success at Marienfeld with "sod farms" of potatoes, beans, peas, cabbage, radishes, and many other vegetables thriving in the freshly-turned earth. According to the newspaper article, the farmers were enjoying a good crop of watermelons, grapevines, and fruit trees with, according to the newspaper article, "most excellent growth."

Father Anastasius had a set of instruments to measure temperature and rainfall and reported that from July 15, 1882, to May 1, 1883, "there was an abundant rain to mature any crop. Total rainfall between May 3 and August 4, 1883 was 7.75 inches. This rainfall on cultivated soil was retained and yielded a greater benefit than on the prairie."

Indeed, the comprehensive reports of the merits of Marienfeld as an opportunity for farming attracted an influx of settlers. Another *Galveston County Daily News* article on January 4, 1884, most likely contributed by a resident, included this charming description of Marienfeld:

> "In the pretty little German settlement of Marienfeld, lying in an endless ocean of green grass, there are forty to fifty neat houses, scattered over several miles of territory. At the railroad station is a general country store, a restaurant, a school, a church, and some fifteen or twenty private houses. Surrounding the station are great tracts of wheat, oats, barley, and rye, all in the deepest green."

It appears that not every family hoping to make a home at Marienfeld was able to make it happen. According to the family history of Gustav Philipp, he sold his house and land in Austria in 1884 and moved his wife and seven children to resettle in Marienfeld. Once the Philipps arrived at the settlement, the farmer was prohibited from buying land because he wasn't Catholic. Instead, the Philipp family began a new life in Midland where they thrived, running a successful dairy for many years.

Another newspaper article later in 1884 in *The Galveston County Daily News* reported a desirable feature of Marienfeld:

> "You do not see a single shanty or mean-looking house anywhere in the settlement. The houses are all neat, tasty, freshly painted, and of a very thrifty aspect. No one can pass the place without conceiving a high opinion of the population. They are now building a convent on a conspicuous eminence, which will present quite an imposing appearance when finished."

Father Anastasius partnered with a farmer and purchased a threshing machine that turned out 700 bushels of high-quality wheat in the summer of 1884. The priest entered a bushel of this crop as well as samples of other Martin County crops in the World's Industrial and Cotton Centennial Exposition at New Orleans, Louisiana. The wheat won a gold medal, and the story of the flourishing West Texas settlement spread.

A lengthy excursion to Marienfeld ending with the First Annual Fair of Martin County was advertised extensively in major newspapers in the fall of 1885. The expedition was scheduled to leave St. Louis and Chicago on November 17 and, traveling on the Texas and Pacific Railway, would "pass Little Rock, Texarkana,

Ribbon and first-place medal from the World's Industrial and Cotton Centennial Exposition in New Orleans, Louisiana, 1884-85. A sample of wheat grown at Marienfeld, Texas won a gold medal at this exposition. *Georgeann Walton.*

Marshall, Longview, Mineola, and Terrell, to Dallas and Fort Worth, thence through Cisco, Abilene, Colorado City, arriving at Marienfeld in the afternoon of the 20th of November, in ample time to thoroughly inspect the agricultural products exhibited at the FIRST ANNUAL FAIR OF MARTIN COUNTY." Round trip "Land Explorer" tickets were offered for sale in "all Coupon Ticket Offices in Iowa, Illinois, Kansas, Indiana, Ohio, Tennessee, Kentucky, Missouri, Michigan, Wisconsin and other States. The Round Trip rate from St. Louis to Marienfeld and return is $38.45. Rates from points in Texas will be quoted by nearest ticket agent." At the fair, Father Anastasius and others aggressively sold town lots.

Newspaper advertisement for Marienfeld town lots, 1885. *Martin County Museum.*

The editor of the *Big Springs Pantagraph* visited Marienfeld to report on this unusual marketing event. He wrote:

"At last, the German settlement was reached, and we alighted to make a thorough inspection of the town, the farms, and the surrounding country. We looked into the room where all the products of the country are exhibited for the benefit of prospectors. Here can be seen corn, wheat, oats, castor beans, wheat in the sheaf, peaches, cucumbers, rice, tobacco, cotton, etc., all grown within a short distance of the depot.

"The principal and largest farms are those of Messrs. Haas and Schaffer, although other parties have equally productive farms, but not conducted on so extensive a scale. Water is plentiful, and nearly every house has a windmill. Mr. J. B. Koonz has a miniature waterworks on his place operating from his windmill, distributing water through his garden, and carrying it to his brother's farm, some distance off. The soil is generally rich and very productive. There are several stores – including a fine drug establishment – a brick-yard, lumber-yard, and a sorghum-mill."

During these very productive days in Martin County, the remote settlement caught the attention of many publications and writers. One Dallas newspaper described the crops surrounding the town as being in "most splendid condition and everybody in the best of spirits." Calling Marienfeld "a snug little town with 600 Germans" surrounded by 30,000 acres farmed by the colonists, the article explained that approximately 8,000 acres were fenced.

Most of the homes were reported to "mostly have stoves made for burning stone coal. Good coal can be bought in car load lots at seven dollars a ton, delivered in Marienfeld. By having short winters in Texas, the coal bills are not extravagant or astonishing large." In one more enticement to recruit settlers, the feature stories usually ended by stating that "in fact the living all the way through is about as cheap as in any of the eastern or northern states." Weather was described as "pure and bracing; the nights are cool."

By the mid-1880s, the development of the community of Marienfeld was reaching a pinnacle, and this success prompted the establishment of a railroad without rails running north 125 miles into the panhandle of Texas to Estacado, a Quaker farming settlement, in Crosby County. Known as the Marienfeld, Estacado and West Texas Steam Transportation, *The Dallas Daily Herald* described the steam-powered conveyance as being organized by the citizens and colonists of Marienfeld.

> "The rolling stock consists of several peculiarly constructed engines and cars, both freight and passenger, intended to run over the ground without the use of rails. An ordinary train of engine and three freights and one passenger car will pull 60,000 pounds of freight. The line of this company passes through the counties of Martin, Dawson, Lynn, Lubbock, and Crosby to the Cox Colony, and extends south of Marienfeld to Centralia station in Tom Green County and thence to San Angelo. At present trips are only made twice a week to Estacado. The rate of speed is from six to eight miles per hour until the road bed is in first-class condition, when swifter engines will be used for passenger traffic."

A trip on this "railroad" at eight miles an hour from Marienfeld to the end of the line in Estacado would take 16 ¼ hours – nonstop. By today's standards, the same trip would take two and a half hours by automobile.

Chapter 4
Carmelite Commitment and Courage

The land was fertile, and the grass grew tall. This was a prosperous time in Martin County for farmers, ranchers, merchants, and the railroad. The Carmelites provided a spiritual foundation for the area. By the time the Martin County government had taken shape, formally established in 1884 with Marienfeld as the county seat, eight priests, eight lay brothers, and as many as forty clerics formed the local Carmelite community.

With more novices for the order expected from Germany, in 1884, the Carmelites began work on a two-story, adobe building to be used as a school for boys, a monastery for the priests and candidates to the priesthood living quarters.

Carmelite historian Father John-Benedict Weber, O.Carm. compiled the following construction chronology:

1884 – Work began on an adobe and wood monastery. Wind storms in June of this year seriously damaged the wood frame church, and construction of an adobe church was underway. Occupied by friars in the autumn of this year.

1885 – Laid cornerstone of new, adobe St. Joseph Church that was built around the original wood-frame church. The adobe walls were veneered with red brick left over from the building of the county courthouse.

1885 – Monastery was initiated as a formed religious house with canonical standing in the Order.

1888 – Additional section of the monastery was built with adobe, ensuring that each friar has his own cell.

A letter from Father Anastasius Peters to Prior General Father Savini in Rome dated March 12, 1885, stated that a building program was initiated after June of 1884. An adobe and wood monastery, 84 ft. long by 28 ft. wide by 19 ft. high, was built in the summer and autumn months. The Marienfeld priest also described wind storms of June 1884 that seriously damaged the wood frame church. An adobe church was under construction to replace the older frame structure.

Anecdotal evidence and oral histories describe the work of Mexican laborers from Ysleta who were brought to Marienfeld to do the highly specialized work of building the large adobe structure of the monastery.

Latin words on a column in St. Joseph Church taken from a 13th century Gregorian chant. *Martin County Museum.*

Historical architect and adobe specialist Paul G. McHenry, Jr. of Albuquerque, New Mexico declared that "the monastery building is a unique example, frozen in time, of the community of Stanton, Texas. Few such examples still exist, and all steps should be taken to preserve this one.

Old photos, mockups and museum exhibits can never provide the same experience as walking through history in the real thing."

Father Anastasius served as the first prior of the monastery and the first pastor of the parish. He also organized and supervised the dissemination of the Catholic faith to other locations in West Texas and southeastern New Mexico. However, in a short time, other priests moved to the settlement to assist. They contributed a positive influence over the spiritual lives of Martin County parishioners as well as a much broader mission field. Clerics studying for the priesthood took courses such as Latin, English, Spanish, and philosophy at the Marienfeld monastery.

The monastery's daily lifestyle followed the Constitutions of the Order that, at the time, were unchanged since the last revision in 1656. These "Rules of Daily Living" dictated a precise schedule followed by priests. The daily schedule or horarium (Latin word meaning "the hours") varied in winter months, when there was less sunlight, from the summer horarium, which provided more time for manual labor, study, and reading. The following is an example of a typical summer horarium. The "choral prayer" times correspond to various times of the day, derived from Psalm 118, verse 164, which states, "Seven times a day I give praise to you."

A replica the Christian relic "Veil of Veronica" in the adobe wall of the main building of Monastery of the Most Pure Heart of Mary. *Martin County Convent Foundation, Inc.*

Martin County Convent Foundation

Rules for Daily Living

TIME	ACTIVITY
12 Midnight	rise
12:15 a.m.	choral prayer of Matins and Prime in chapel
1:30 a.m.	retire
6:00 a.m.	rise
6:15 a.m.	choral prayer of Lauds in chapel, followed by meditation
7:00 a.m.	conventual Mass in chapel (8:00 a.m. on Sundays)
7:45 a.m.	choral prayer of Terce in chapel
8:00 a.m.	classes, or manual labor (Sundays: reading, study, walk, letter writing, personal prayer)
11:45 a.m.	choral prayer of Sext in chapel
12:00 Noon	dinner in refectory (accompanied by scriptural or devotional reading aloud)
12:30 p.m.	choral prayer of None in chapel
12:45 p.m.	free time or community recreation
2:00 p.m.	Study time or manual labor (Sundays: reading, study, walk, letter writing, personal prayer, or spiritual conference in common)
5:15 p.m.	choral prayer of Vespers in chapel, followed by meditation (Sundays: followed by Benediction)
6:00 p.m.	Supper in refectory
6:30 p.m.	study or free time
7:30 p.m.	rosary, examination of conscience and choral prayer of Compline in chapel
8:00 p.m.	study, or reading, or retire
9:00 p.m.	retire

Despite the decline of Marienfeld in other ways, in 1889, the Monastery of the Most Pure Heart of Mary reached its peak as a Carmelite religious house with seven Solemnly Professed priests in residence, 17 Simply Professed, and 10 Novices. Two years later, only five Solemnly Professed and two Simply Professed priests remained at the monastery.

The spiritual responsibilities of the priests of Marienfeld extended beyond Martin County to the vast area of West Texas and southeastern New Mexico. A document held at the Catholic Archives of Texas describes the Carmelite missions extending from the Colorado River on the east to the Rio Grande River on the west; thence north to Eddy (now Carlsbad), New Mexico, and Brogardo, Texas on the south.

Carmelite priests, Monastery of the Most Pure Heart of Mary, Marienfeld, Texas ca. 1890: (seated l to r) Rev. Joseph Walsh, Rev. Alphonse Brondstaltter, Rev. Al-bert Wagner. (standing l to r) Bro. Baptist Goar, Bro. Victor Heilmeyer, Bro. Bonoventure Tenhoof, Bro. Elias Maurer, Bro. Angelus Augustine Maurer. *Martin County Foundation, Inc.*

Rev. Simon Weeg, O.C.C., known as Father Simon, was a well-regarded member of the Carmelite community at the Marienfeld monastery between 1886 and 1898, serving as rector from 1893 to 1898. He was responsible for much of the growth of the Carmelite mission into New Mexico. The Carmelites established additional New Mexico mission stations along the Pecos Valley Railroad, including Malaga, Red Bluff, Roswell, Seven Rivers, and Loving. After Father Simon left Marienfeld, he was a chaplain at St. Regis' House, the Convent of Our Lady of the Cenacle in Queens, New York. He passed away on September 21, 1901, and is buried in the Carmelite cemetery at Englewood, New Jersey.

Spiritual service among the Mexican and immigrant farming communities along the railroad required much travel by the Marienfeld priests along a 200-mile stretch of the Texas and Pacific Railway. The vast distances often meant the priests were away for weeks at a time. Although the railroad issued train passes for the priests, often, the train did not reach these remote settlements. These situations required a priest to travel by horse or wagon through treacherous territory, often in extreme seasonal weather. Yet, the Carmelite priests saw this as fertile spiritual ground and remained loyal to their calling.

Establishing a spiritual foundation in far West Texas also proved to be difficult because of the poverty of most of the Catholics who had settled in the area. Financial reports during the first years of the monastery at Marienfeld show that the parishioners altogether gave approximately $50 each Sunday, and the other mission stations together "netted the friars only about $300 annually." Father Boniface reported: "Our income, besides the fruits of the fields cultivated by our lay brothers… there are Mass stipends, collections from the missions besides gifts of the Leopoldine Society of Vienna and the Society of St. Louis." (These organizations supported Catholic missions in North America.) Another report describes the Carmelite mission as having an area of about 1,700 square miles. The mission efforts were challenging "since a priest could not visit people monthly, and since there is no chapel, often Mass is celebrated in the humble homes of parishioners." No doubt a visit from a priest was a welcome spiritual salve to these distant parishioners.

According to historian Father John-Benedict Weber, by 1895, "the Carmelites administered from Marienfeld to roughly 5,000 people at 35 mission stations in West Texas and southeast New Mexico. Many times, these missionaries were on the move from station-to-station weeks at a time, with hardly a rest period at the monastery. The constant travel, by demand of their overwhelming missionary apostolate, greatly weakened the community spirit at the monastery and even hindered the education of the younger friars at Marienfeld. Tending to the spiritual needs of a diverse population – German, Scotch-Irish, Swiss, and Mexican – who lived in places that varied from small farming or mining settlements to large and lawless cow towns, necessitated great understanding and even raw courage on the part of the Carmelite missionaries." Clearly, the priests possessed a deep commitment to their life's work.

A priest who studied at the monastery in the late 1880s told a story that gives an example of the fatigue as well as the spiritual benefits of travel. Regardless of circumstances, mission work was ever-present.

> "Our Father Prior of Marienfeld, Simon Weeg, returned home from a far trip on the Texas & Pacific Railway. The stations are all alike – simple frame-buildings and the country around them the same plane [sic]. It was a dark evening, when he left the train with his mission satchel at the wrong station. Before he noticed his error, the conductor called out: 'All aboard,' and the train was gone. One hundred miles away from Marienfeld, only the train every 24 hours in each direction, what could he do, but go to the little town and look for a room in a boarding house.
>
> "When the landlady placed the book before him to sign his name, she was surprised to read: Father Simon Weeg, Carmelite priest. She was no Catholic, and no Catholics in the town."

The woman was surprised to see a priest at her boarding house. She explained to Father Weeg that she had a guest in the house who was dying and begging her to bring him a Catholic priest. No one in town knew of any priests, and Fr. Weeg had arrived just in time to minister to the boarder.

"She led Father Simon to the room of the dying man, and you may imagine the joy of the poor man when he saw that God's Providence sent him a priest in such a puzzling way. Father Simon heard his confession and, in the morning, said Mass in the room of the patient. His mission satchel contained all he needed for this purpose.

Wonderful are the ways of Providence!"

By 1890, although the population of Marienfeld had greatly declined, the monastery had grown in importance to Texas and surrounding states, prompting further initiative to increase the reach of the Catholic faith. For a time, the Monastery of the Most Pure Heart of Mary served as headquarters for three other monasteries in Louisiana and West Texas, organized within the Carmelite Order and known as the Commissariat of the South.

Chapter 5
Nature Does Not Make Her a Paradise

The rapid growth and success of early Marienfeld concealed the lack of knowledge on the part of the new inhabitants about West Texas weather and climate. No one was prepared for the drought of 1886 - 1888 or the vicious winter blizzards of 1887 - 88 that very nearly destroyed the colony. The majority of the settlers were German immigrants who relied on their native farming practices and economic traditions. While this brought the farmers success in their native land and during the first years on the Staked Plains, these methods could not sustain them through a lengthy drought.

"I said Marienfeld was a prosperous town," former Marienfeld priest Father Telesphorus wrote in his remembrances, "but only as long as no drought set in. Nobody knew on these vast prairies – staked planes [sic] – that I belong to is a so-called rainless zone. When the drought set in, we waited for rain fully eighteen months; sand storms, which we called Texas rain, were frequent occurrences. No grass grew on the planes [sic], cattle and sheep starving."

A special report dispatched to the *Fort Worth Daily Gazette* on April 14, 1887, provides this description of a slight but welcome respite from the drought at Marienfeld:

"For several days a sand storm has been blowing from the south and often bringing little pebbles with it. At 4:00 p.m. we saw clouds coming from the northwest, and it looked as though the sand hills, clear down to the rocks, were coming down on us. Mothers and children were afraid their time had come, and day was turned to night, when lo and behold the rain began and the clouds of sand had to submit and lay themselves to rest and day began to dawn again and everybody began to wear a smile, thanking God the drought has been broken by a good shower of rain."

Main street of early Marienfeld, Texas. *Martin County Museum.*

Six days later, Marienfeld reported more rain to the *Gazette* along with a plea for cottonseed to plant immediately. "Seed corn has been furnished to the farmers, but there is not a pound of cottonseed in the county." By mid-May, more rain had fallen, and "waterholes are all full, and we can say verily the good old time has come again. Rev. P.A. Peters [Father Anastasius Peters] is putting in irrigation pipes, he is going to purchase pumps for his wells. Our real estate is taking a boom." Again, it appears that this "news" story was probably written either by Father

Anastasius or A. Rawlins, owner of the *Marienfeld News*. Regardless of the glowingly optimistic reports, these rains were not enough to break the drought and revive the hopeful future of Marienfeld.

The Carmelite brothers were not immune to the adverse effects of the extreme weather. The priests sold 800 acres of their 2,000-acre farm to pay their debts and purchase food and supplies. Many of the original families who had helped establish the town abandoned the area.

An agricultural report released in 1890 described Martin County and the Staked Plains as having its drawbacks adding that "men view her with superstition because nature does not make her a paradise."

Despite this downward turn of events, an optimistic Father Anastasius partnered with some Dallas-area investors and founded the Marienfeld Fruit Growing, Gardening, and Irrigation Company. Frank E. Roesler, an emigration agent of the Texas and Pacific Railway, served as secretary of the company. The Secretary of State of Texas' Biennial Report lists the company as a domestic for-profit company with capital stock of $25,000 in May 1888. The company goals were "to grow fruits, vegetables and general farm crops by irrigation," to "market the products grown." The company also planned "to promote horticulture, agriculture, vine growing, and general farming in Martin and adjoining counties in Texas." Eventually, the company hoped to develop a widespread irrigation system by digging wells, installing windmills, and building dams and tanks to furnish a dependable water supply for the company and other local users.

Texas Farm & Ranch published an article by "Light Horse" Harry Love in 1889 describing his trip to visit the Marienfeld Fruit Growing company:

"While this is the entrance to that drought-stricken region, known as the staked plains, it poured down rain for the next six or eight hours after my arrival so that I could do nothing but wait for another drought in order to take a look at the country.

I visited the farm of a thrifty, and the most intelligent Bohemian whom I have met. He landed upon this spot of ground with barely means sufficient to take the necessary steps in settling a homestead, some three years since, and has not only made a good living, but has converted this piece of raw prairie, partially covered with mesquite, and inhabited by prairie dogs, into a comfortable home; surrounded with the necessaries of life, and many a vineyard containing seven hundred grapevines which are now one and a half years old and doing as well as he could wish.

"While at Marienfeld I visited the convent, presided over by Father [Anastasius] Peters whom I found to be a genial and well-preserved old gentleman, and an enthusiast in vine culture. Here I found hundreds of vines representing many varieties, loaded down with grapes from which Father Peters gave me a warm reception and a glass of wine of his own manufacture from last year's vintage. While I am a novice in this line, I do claim to know a good thing when I taste it, and I have no hesitation in saying that this was the most palatable wine that I ever drank.

The Marienfeld Fruit Growing, Gardening, and Irrigation Company's well-intentioned efforts to foster an ongoing, thriving agriculture region were not successful. The company's charter was allowed to lapse in 1895.

Martin County, Texas would not become the utopia that Father Anastasius and others hoped for and believed possible. The West Texas winds brought more than sand. The winds of change were sweeping across the settlement; the culture and leadership were shifting. With most German settlers leaving to find other opportunities to make a living, by 1890, most of the residents were non-German. By referendum, the citizens changed the name of the settlement to Stanton. At this time, the Martin County census had shrunk to 264 from a peak population of 450 to 500 residents. Only 136 were considered residents of Stanton. According to the 1890 U.S.

Census Office, only 48 of the Martin County residents claimed a foreign birth. During the previous eight years, immediately following the arrival of the Carmelites, the majority of the residents had been foreign-born. The predominantly agriculturally oriented German-Catholic population had been replaced by a ranching-oriented Anglo-Saxon Protestant population.

Not all of the original German settlers moved away from the community. Some dug in, survived the treacherous West Texas weather, and enjoyed long, productive lives in Martin County. Ignatius George "Ick" Peters, Sr. is an example of these men. The fifth of eight children born to Jacob and Margaretha Peters, Ignatius was the first and the only draftee from Martin County to go into World War I because the draft specified only five percent of the eligible men. According to the Peters family history, he fought in France and was sent to Germany in the occupation army. Ignatius was discharged in June of 1919 and returned to Martin County, where he married Maria Anna "Mary Ann" Straub in 1924. Ignatius was "a self-taught soil conservationist…interested in improvement of the soil in all ways, agriculturally and scientifically." He was nominated for 1976 Outstanding Older Texan for Martin County and received recognition at the state capitol in Austin. Ignatius was also a charter member of the Char-Swiss Cattle Association of Texas.

At the end of 1891, there were only five priests in residence at the Monastery of the Most Pure Heart of Mary with Father Albert Wagner as both prior and pastor. Bishop Neraz of the San Antonio Diocese, who had greatly assisted the relocation of Father Anastasius and other Carmelite priests to Texas, offered the remaining Carmelites a larger mission territory in far southwest Texas along the border with Mexico. In 1892, Father Wagner transferred to Fort Davis, Texas, where he served as pastor of St. Joseph parish.

In eight years, the Catholic colony of Marienfeld had failed. During the ensuing years, the priests moved to various parishes throughout Texas, with some returning to Europe, where they secured the Marian Shrine church at Maria Taferl in Austria. Father Weber remarked in his writing that "with the same vigor and enthusiasm they had displayed in Texas pursuing their religious life and ministry as missionaries, the Marienfeld friars began to reestablish the Carmelites in Austria-Hungry."

In an article for the *Journal of Texas Catholic History and Culture,* Father Weber wrote:

Father Albert Wagner served at the Marienfeld monastery 1885 – 1902.
Martin County Museum.

"The original goal for which the Peters brothers established the Carmelites at Marienfeld did not long materialize. The German Catholic colony was not successful. The presence of the friars in West Texas proved elusive and came to an end at their own hands because of issues of personality, economy, and authority. What did remain of the Carmelites in West Texas and what proved of enduring value was the nurturing of the Christian faith in the Catholic peoples the friars served in very diverse and distant towns and settlements throughout West Texas."

The failure of the Marienfeld settlement as a thriving farming community and religious center must have been especially difficult for Father Anastasius. His influence in attempting to bring families to the settlement was paramount, and occasionally, in Texas newspapers, Marienfeld was called "Father Peters' German colony" or said to be "presided over by Father

P.A. Peters." Frank Roesler, with the Texas and Pacific Railway, posed an alternative rationale for the failure of Marienfeld in an 1890 report to the U.S. Senate Select Committee on Irrigation and Reclamation of Arid Lands. He believed the failure of the settlement was beyond the realm of mere mortals. "It does not appear that such crop failures as have been encountered were due in full measure to a lack of precipitation, but rather to the want of discretion on part of the Rainmaker in a proper distribution of the same. The conditions of the precipitation in Texas are peculiar and well defined."

The Marienfeld Carmelites published this notice in the San Antonio *Southern Messenger*, the first statewide Catholic newspaper in Texas:

> "Notice to Rev. Clergy: As the Carmelite Fathers are going to leave Texas, the reverend clergy are requested to send the names of those enrolled in the Holy Scapular to some other Carmelite monastery.
> Carmelite Fathers, Stanton, Texas"

Late in 1888, Father Anastasius began to separate from the Marienfeld community and, with several other Carmelites, moved part-time to Bayou Pierre, near Mansfield, Louisiana. Eventually, Father Anastasius was appointed commissary general of the Commissariat of the South and was also appointed the United States postmaster of Bayou Pierre. As early as 1892, Father Anastasius' family was aware that his health was deteriorating. Two years later, the priest resigned and moved to Thurber, Texas, where he was a local superior for a brief time. In 1895, Fathers Anastasius and Boniface left America and settled at Maria Taferl, southwest of Vienna, Austria. Father Anastasius Peters, the visionary who established a farming community and a monastery in desolate West Texas, died on February 16, 1912, and is buried in Ybbsitz, Austria. The priest was 68 years old. His brother, Father Boniface, who worked alongside him to establish the German Catholic colony, preceded Fr. Anastasius in death in 1902.

Holy Card for Father Anastasius. The priest who founded the Monastery of the Most Pure Heart of Mary died February 16, 1912. *Martin County Museum.*

Chapter 6
Death at the Monastery

A shocking event at the monastery may have had an adverse effect on the cultural climate in Martin County, almost to the extent that the severe weather drove many German settlers away. Even though there were actual incidents of horse thieves and wanted men who passed through this mostly uncivilized country, the spurious rumors surrounding the death of a young monk at the Monastery of the Most Pure Heart of Mary were particularly damaging to the German-Catholic population.

A report by Father J. O. Sirius, O.M.I., based on his interviews with individuals who were part of the investigation into the death by suicide of a postulant at the Marienfeld monastery, provides an accurate accounting of the facts of the event.

The student monk, Lawrence Esser, was also known as Brother Francis and sometimes called Brother Franz. He was 19 years old at the time of his death in 1888. Research by Father John-Benedict Weber indicates that the young man left a suicide note, but because of the personal information, "the Order does not want it made public because it reflects badly on him."

Father Sirius wrote:

"In the spring of 1888, a student monk, Lawrence Esser, committed suicide by hanging himself in his cell [on the second floor of the monastery]. An inquest was held by Adam Konz, Justice of the Peace, and a verdict of suicide was rendered. The body was buried in the northwest corner of the cemetery in a plot reserved for non-Catholics, without Christian burial.

"About a month after the suicide, another student, Richard Maier, aged 26, left the community and went to Midland to work on a cattle ranch. He told his boss that the young man, Esser, had been murdered. The boss, a Freemason, notified his lodge, and this lodge started an investigation before Ethan Allen, County Judge of Martin County. The body [Esser] was exhumed, and Dr. S. E. Price of Big Spring held an autopsy and declared that death had been caused by strangulation. At that time the monastery was in the charge of Rev. Andrew Fuhrwerk as sub-prior, Rev. P.A. Peters being in Louisiana. Judge Allen held an examining trial and Andrew Fuhrwerk was formally charged with murder and Adam Konz; both were put on a one-thousand-dollar bond to await action of the Grand Jury in October.

"In the meantime, Rev. Fuhrwerk was transferred to Castroville [Texas] as Chaplain of the Sisters of Divine Providence.

"Two months after an officer of the Masonic Lodge at Midland made affidavit before Judge Allen that new evidence had been found. Judge Allen issued warrants for Fuhrwerk and Konz. A deputy sheriff was sent to Castroville, who arrested Fuhrwerk and brought him back here [Martin County]. His attorney sued out of writ of Habeas Corpus before Judge Wm. Kennedy at Colorado City, who ordered both to be brought before him. After the hearing Judge Kennedy decided that the new evidence was immaterial and ordered that the defendants be held under the original bonds for the Grand Jury.

"In October the Grand Jury investigated the case and exhonerated [sic] Rev. Fuhrwerk, but indicted Konz for malfaisance [sic] in office, alleging that Konz failed to report the inquest as directed by law. At the next term of the District Court…the case was tried again before Judge Kennedy without jury. After hearing, the Judge ruled that Adam Konz had made his report in time and entered a judgment of not guilty and ordered Konz discharged."

Father Anastasius Peters later wrote from Louisiana that, although he was thankful for the acquittal, the trial dramatically affected the priests in Marienfeld both emotionally and financially, costing "us poor monks five hundred dollars."

Fortunately, we have this personal statement by Father Sirius from the Catholic Archives of Texas to provide the facts from witnesses of the circumstances surrounding the young student monk's death. Unfortunately, the story attracted national attention and was, and in some instances continues to be, sensationalized. A short article appeared in *The New York Times* on October 12, 1889, with the headline, "A Boy's Strange Story." The piece implied that Esser was a student at the boy's school at the monastery and stated that a fellow student "escaped and told a story of an alleged murder by two priests who, along with four students, secretly buried the body." A similar article in the *Daily Alta California* newspaper appeared on the same date with an added, erroneous line stating that the priests of Marienfeld had committed other murders.

At the time of the young man's burial in the cemetery adjacent to the monastery, the grave was left unmarked. A marker was placed later, but with incorrect dates.

Chapter 7
Schooling Comes to the Staked Plains

A report by Most Rev. Laurence J. FitzSimon, D.D., Bishop of Amarillo, written in 1947, states that in 1887 the Carmelite monastery founded a parochial school at Marienfeld, and nuns with the Sisters of Divine Providence of San Antonio were placed in charge. At this time, the sisters also hoped to establish a hospital.

These sisters were particularly suited to develop a school in this remote area of Texas. The group was a branch of the institute founded in 1762 by John Martin Moye in Lorraine, France, to educate poor children, particularly in "country" places. The first overseas mission of the congregation was in 1866. Superior St. Andrew Feltin and Sister Alphonse Boegler traveled from France to Galveston, Texas, answering the call of Father Claude Dubuis, the Bishop of Galveston, to establish schools in the rural towns of his diocese. The following year, the sisters opened a school in Austin, the first parochial school in Texas under the Sisters of Divine Providence's auspices. According to the Congregation of Divine Providence website, "Immediately, work started in founding schools in the Castroville area as young women joined the fledgling congregation.

Requests came from pastors all over Texas, and later from Louisiana and Oklahoma, for sisters to open schools in their parishes. There were also settlements without churches, far from towns, in need of literacy and God's Word." This 1882 entry in the diary of Sister Catherine Friesenhahn, one of the nuns helping establish the rural Texas schools, provides a hint of how difficult this work was:

> "Our house was poor and exercise was not wanting. We had to take a regular good long walk each day to go after water. We also learned how to split the wood for fire to prepare our meals. A man would cut down the tree but left it to us to make it fit for the kitchen. Many were our hardships."

Within ten years, Sisters of Divine Providence had established schools throughout central and west Texas, including Fredericksburg, New Braunfels, and Galveston. Around the same time that the sisters came to Marienfeld in 1887, the group was also opening schools in Louisiana, "including five schools for Black children and, a few years later, in Oklahoma, including several for Indian children." In a written history of the Sisters of Divine Providence work, Sister M. Claude Lane, O.P., reports that "…in 1910, the order was located in two archdioceses and six dioceses and was operating 69 academies and schools with a combined enrollment of nearly 10,000 children." An 1895 newspaper advertisement for the school established by the Sisters of Divine Providence in Galveston describes what their schools offered students: "…The course of studies is systematic and affords a thorough education in English and German. The number of children which has always attended the school is sufficient proof of the competency of the sisters and the parental care which is manifested toward them. Children of both sexes from five years of age are received. Great care is given to forming the morals and manners of the pupils. Music, drawing, painting and fancy work receive special attention. For further particulars address Sister Superior."

Mother Superior Sister Teresa oversaw the school operations at Marienfeld; Sister Mary Angela taught German and English, and Sister Agatha taught needlework. Sister Adelheid took care of the household, and during the second year at the school, Sister Yodoka taught music.

In the 1983 *Panhandle-Plains Historical Review*, Don Abbe writes that, as a result of "the drought of 1886 – 1888, both the farms of Martin County and the schools wilted away." By 1889 the situation had become so serious that the school, supervised by the capable Sisters of Divine Providence, could not survive. "The seminary students [clerics] transferred to a new Carmelite venture in Louisiana. The Sisters of Divine Providence persevered for four years, but they finally admitted defeat in 1891 and closed the school."

Although the Sisters of Divine Providence only operated the school for a short time, the educational center at Marienfeld would open again and survive for many years as the only Catholic academy between Fort Worth and El Paso.

Chapter 8
A Thorough and Refined Education

Mother Superior of Academy	Dates Served
Sister M. Berchmans Kast	1894 - 1913
Sister M. Angela Hoestetter	1913 - 1921
Sister M. Stanislaus Broderick	1921 – 1928
Sister M. Columba Salmon	1929 - 1934
Sister M. Aloysius DuBronz	1934 - 1938

Sisters of Mercy nuns would sustain the convent and school in Martin County for over 40 years. The Order was founded in Dublin, Ireland, in 1831, by Catherine Elizabeth McCauley, an Irish Catholic laywoman who determined that she and women like her could make a difference in the lives of economically poor people. Catherine first established a place to shelter and educate women and girls. The Archbishop of Dublin was impressed by her good works and realized the importance of continuity in the ministry. He advised her to establish a religious congregation, and three years later, Catherine and two companions became the first Sisters of Mercy. By the mid-20th century, the Sisters of Mercy had grown to be the second largest order in the world. Nuns from the Sisters of Mercy Order first arrived in the United States from Ireland in 1843. They began work in Texas in 1875, transferring to Indianola, on Matagorda Bay, from their St. Patrick Convent of Mercy in New Orleans.

In a 1947 report, the Most Rev. Laurence J. FitzSimon, D.D., Bishop of Amarillo, gives homage to the influence of the Sisters of Mercy and their service at Stanton:

> "In reality only the academy at Stanton gives continuity to the history of the Sisters in the area of the Diocese, but even that once flourishing institution is today but a memory. Yet it must be added that the Sisters of Mercy in the Diocese of Amarillo have retained the wealth of a fine spiritual heritage that is shared by many who years ago learnt from them the first rudiments of religion and who are today active and devoted members of several parishes in the Diocese. Wherever the Sisters once labored, their zeal and example have been an enduring source of edification and have contributed greatly to the strengthening of the Faith in communities where Catholics have had a battle against prejudice and hostility."

Mother Superior Mary Berchmans Kast, founder of Our Lady of Mercy Academy and Convent, Marienfeld, Texas. *Martin County Foundation, Inc.*

According to the Most Rev. FitzSimon, "On the 9th of March, 1894, under the leadership of Sister M. Berchmans Kast, a small group of Sisters of Mercy from St. Mary's Hospital of San Francisco, California, arrived at Stanton, Martin County in West Texas. The town of Stanton then with a population of about 200."

The parochial school founded a decade earlier by the Carmelite priests reopened with 16 students attending. The Sisters of Mercy originally rented the facilities from the Carmelite priests, and three years later, the priests sold the entire Marienfeld complex to the sisters. Several sources document that Mother Berchmans' brother, Louis Kast, purchased the property from the Carmelite monastery for the Sisters of Mercy.

In 1897, the Mother Superior began a large building program creating a compound with an inner court that opened to the south, toward the town of Stanton. Two windmills with cisterns supplied water. To the rear of the main buildings were several smaller structures, one of which was a laundry. Carbide lights provided illumination, and for many years there was no indoor plumbing. The Academy of Our Lady of Mercy formally opened in the fall of that year with 61 pupils.

Early students at Our Lady of Mercy Academy, Marienfeld, Texas. Date unknown. *University of North Texas Libraries, The Portal to Texas History, https://texashistory.unt.edu; crediting Texas Historical Commission.*

MARTIN COUNTY CONVENT FOUNDATION

In her book, *Journeys: A Pre-Amalgamation History of the Sisters of Mercy*, Kathleen O'Brien, R.S.M. relates details about a fortuitous meeting that led to the formation of Our Lady of Mercy Academy and Convent:

"In 1894, Sister Berchmans Kast, returning to California after visiting family in the eastern United States, stopped in El Paso where she and two sisters accompanying her met a German Carmelite Monk [Fr. Simon Weeg] who served in Marienfeld, Texas, with the German immigrants who had settled there.

"Fr. Weeg was surprised and pleased to discover that Sister Berchmans could speak fluent German. He pressed upon the Sister the great need at Marienfeld. Sr. Berchmans agreed to place the mission possibility before her superior in San Francisco and, if she agreed, Sr. Berchmans would recruit volunteers to come with her to Texas. On March 9, 1894, she began her apostolate in Marienfeld.

"…the Mercy community was founded in 1894 under the patronage of Father Simon Weeg, Prior of the Carmelite monastery and Mrs. Pat Durack of Barstow, Texas, a benefactor of the fledgling Catholic ministries in Texas. At first, there was no convent for the Sisters, and they moved into a private residence in the town. It seems that it was not until after they arrived that they [the Sisters] made arrangements with the bishop, John C. Neraz of San Antonio.

"Although the religious house received ample material help when her wealthy family sent a train car load of furniture and supplies in 1895, most of the sisters who came to Marienfeld with Sr. Berchmans were not happy in Texas. Several returned to California, leaving the academy with very little staff. Sr. Berchmans returned to San Francisco that year to recruit more sisters for the new foundation."

The likely reason a new mission in remote West Texas was appealing to Sister Berchmans is explained in correspondence from Sr. Mary Beata Bauman, Sisters of Mercy in California, concerning research for a book she and Sr. Cecelia Mary Barry, Sisters of Mercy Historical Researcher in Oregon were writing. "Her [Sr. Berchmans'] younger sister was also in our community. The only comment on her record is that she [the younger sister] left. The circumstances surrounding the departure was a scandal, I suppose one would say." Later accounts of this time state that Sr. Berchmans' younger sister, Sr. Mary Evangelist, left the Sisters of Mercy of San Francisco to marry. To someone as dedicated to her mission, as was the case with Sister Berchmans, this situation was especially difficult. "This led to the older member of the family choosing to leave the San Francisco area. At the time, Sr. Berchmans Kast was in good standing in the religious community with the chapter's approval, the permission of the Superior, and the sanction of the Archbishop of San Francisco." Before coming to Stanton, Sister Berchmans served approximately nine years caring for male orphans at St. Patrick's Orphanage, Grass Valley, California, approximately 50 miles northeast of Sacramento.

During her return trip to California, Sister Berchmans "recruited 26-year-old Helena Hoestetter (later Sister Mary Angela) who was then 26 years old and a dynamic apostolic worker with the Paulist Fathers in San Francisco. She went to school at the Sisters of Mercy St. Peter's Academy and seemed to have acquired her excellent musical training there." With this experience in Sister Angela's early years, no doubt the Stanton academy students received a first-rate education in music, vocals, and piano. Hoestetter family history indicates that young Helena Hoestetter wanted "desperately to be a physician, but her mother objected greatly to a woman, her daughter especially, undertaking such a career in the 1890s. The nursing, medical traits, and desire to care for others always seemed strong in Sister Angela." Some Catholic historians consider Sister Angela a co-founder of Our Lady of Mercy in Stanton. They believe the foundation survived and eventually flourished because of the combination of Sister Angela's acumen and the financial security provided by Sister Berchmans' wealthy family.

The Most Rev. FitzSimon describes the Martin County landscape that greeted the sisters as:

> "...a dreary wasteland, with small scattered communities here and there plagued by drought and dust storms, and barely able to sustain themselves from the products of the farm or ranch. The main floor of the building that would house the academy and, eventually its boarding students, had dirt floors, and the second floor was poorly constructed. There was at least one incident of a nun losing her balance and falling through the floor, landing safely on the dirt floor below, unhurt.
>
> "Spiritual encouragement was lacking, for frequently the local pastor had to be absent on distant missionary calls. Weekday Mass and Communion for the Sisters was a rare privilege. But the Sisters, with admirable patience, taught their classes, often composed of the most unruly children of the western plains."

A legal notice in the *Galveston News* on July 13, 1897, announced "the charter of the Sisters of Mercy educational society of Texas was filed today. No capital stocks. Purposes: support and protection of schools, education, charity and benevolence. Place of business at Stanton, Martin county. Incorporators, Mother Mary Berchmans Kast, Sisters Mary Angela Hoestetter and Mary Magdalen Reikowsky." (The Articles of Corporation, Appendix II) By-laws of the Sisters of Mercy Educational Society of Texas were filed for record on November 16, 1906, and were recorded in Martin County Miscellaneous Record. (By-laws, Appendix III)

Very soon, more teachers were needed at the Academy of Our Lady of Mercy. Sister Berchmans sent two sisters to Ireland to obtain recruits. The sisters returned to Texas with seven sisters who immediately completed their religious training and joined the teaching staff.

Group of nuns who came to the academy from Ireland in 1912: (back row l to r) Sisters Brigid Lyons, Augustine Healy, Joseph Walsh, Columba Salmon. (front row l to r) Sisters Xavier Price, Antonio Reynolds, Cecilia Fleming, Magdalene Broderick. *Martin County Museum*

By 1904, the academy's enrollment reached 110, and for the next 20 years, enrollment remained constant at around 100 students. Most were boarders who lived at the convent while attending classes with hometown addresses in Big Spring, Midland, and Odessa. A testament to the school's good reputation were students who came from towns further away, including Plainview, San Angelo, Fort Stockton, Lubbock, Slaton, and Post. Out-of-state students were often part of the mix, including those from Arizona, California, Oklahoma, and Ohio. The nuns at the academy brought cultural sensibilities to Martin County from Ireland, Germany and Mexico as well as California and New York. The school became known as a proper finishing school for young ladies, emphasizing music, art, and religion. During this time, finishing schools were popular as a place for young girls to receive an education and polish their manners and demeanor.

Because Sister Angela Hoestetter had a familial connection with the prominent twentieth-century marine artist William A. Coulter, students at the academy received high-level art instruction during the 1906 - 07 school year. Hattie Hoestetter Coulter, sister of Sister Angela, was married to the artist and the Coulter family found refuge in Stanton from the aftermath of the devastating 1906 San Francisco earthquake. William and Hattie lived with a family in town. Their three children boarded at the academy and attended classes there. Mr. Coulter taught art to academy students. The esteemed artist also painted the convent chapel during this time. Sister Angela had a piano sent to the school from San Francisco by her brother. The baby grand piano is remembered by many students and was only used for special performances.

Sister Angela, who established herself as a charismatic leader and efficient businesswoman at Our Lady of Mercy, left the academy to begin a foundation in Raton, New Mexico in 1922. The piano remained in the great room of the academy until the school closed. It was then moved to the Community Room of Mercy Hospital in Slaton, Texas.

The sisters at Our Lady of Mercy Academy and Convent didn't wait for students to come to them. They often placed advertisements for the school in the local newspaper and newspapers across the state. A 1908 ad in the *Stanton Reporter* is an example of these marketing efforts:

> "A boarding and day school for young ladies and girls, also boys under ten years of age. Every facility is offered for acquiring a thorough and refined education. The course of study embraces every advantage in the Primary, Intermediate, Academics, Commercial and Musical Department. For catalog and particulars, address Sisters of Mercy, Stanton, TX."

While the nuns established a Catholic school with an excellent reputation, non-Catholics in the area often viewed the academy and convent and its residents as mysterious. When 93-year-old Blythe Weaver Schulze read an article in the *Fort Worth Star-Telegram* featuring plans for the restoration of the surviving building at Stanton, she shared some of her childhood memories:

"My parents, younger brother and I moved in a covered wagon to Stanton where our father would be Superintendent of Stanton schools – about 1905 – and lived there until 1910. The Convent was in operation at that time. Stanton was a small ranch town. I heard my father say that the population shifted…families moved to town during the school year and back to the ranch during vacations.

"The Convent was a landmark on a rise overlooking the town. The nuns in their black robes could be seen walking back and forth along the upper gallery. I never saw them any other place. I cannot recall that there was much relationship between the Convent and town. This from the viewpoint of a child, remember. Practically all the people we knew were Protestants and had reservations about Catholics. The nuns in their black robes were different, mysterious, akin to people in some of the stories read to children – having no part in my real life.

"And then one afternoon my brother and I were playing in the dirt – digging, if my memory does not fail me – and did not see the man coming down the road until he stopped and came over to us. He said in a kindly voice that he was 'Father Hobin.' Hoe-bin was what I understood. I have not heard the name since. It may have been 'Hogan' or some other like-sounding name. He took an interest in what we were making or digging – and opened a package and – wonder of WONDERS – gave us a toy pail and matching shovel – new and brightly colored.

"My brother and I were holding the toys – staring open-mouthed – as he went away down the road. We knew – either from the black suit or perhaps he told us – that he lived at the Convent – which took its place in our imaginations as The-Castle-on-the-Hill.

"This impression was strengthened when a little girl at school told me about one of the women-in-black [the nuns]. The baby at her house had been very ill. Her parents feared he would die. Then one of the women-in-black-robes came with a big pan of medicine. Her description sounded like ointment of some kind. The woman-in-black placed the entire baby's body in the medicine. The baby got well. There must have been many other such Angel-of-Mercy cases."

In 1913, the Stanton Sisters of Mercy opened some of the earliest parochial schools in West Texas, including at Pecos, Big Spring, Fort Stockton, and Menard. These schools were not sustainable, with most poorly built and equipped. The income received by the sisters in these remote locations was described as a mere pittance and their living conditions primitive. A dozen years after these schools opened, all were closed.

When the Sisters of Mercy were increasing the number of parochial schools in Texas, the severe conditions of developing and maintaining Our Lady of Mercy were taking a toll on the nuns who served there. Supervising the children who boarded at the academy and providing spiritual instruction, a clean environment, and three meals a day was taxing enough. Also, the Sisters were responsible for planning and teaching primary through high school classes for boarding and day students. All of this occurred in a compound of several buildings with no electricity or running water. Electric lights replaced carbide and kerosene lamps and gas heating was installed in three buildings and the laundry in 1927. Hard, manual labor was a distinct characteristic of the Mercy way of life in Stanton. The family of Sister Magdalen Broderick, who came to the academy in 1896, visited her three years later and were shocked by her decline. "The twenty-four-year-old woman, who had been robust and healthy when they last saw her, was shrunken – skin and bone," they said. Sr. Magdalen Broderick died of tuberculosis in 1905, but her family believed that she was "a martyr to the life work she had chosen." She died, they believed, of overwork. Sister Magdalen is buried in St. Joseph Cemetery in Stanton.

Chapter 9
Accredited Edification and Enrichment

Sister Aloysius DuBronz, the last Mother Superior to serve at Stanton, wrote this description of life at the academy and convent:

"For many years during this time, the sisters were responsible for milking six Jersey cows owned by the academy. The milk, butter, and cream produced were stored in a small room adjacent to the kitchen which had concrete vats with running water. We also raised chickens and ducks. On the grounds were about 20 or more hives of bees scattered here and there. About twice a year the hives would be robbed and honey placed in a large extractor where the honey was extracted. We usually got 300 gallons or so. The extractor had to be manipulated by hand.

"A Maytag washer was bought for the laundry [the mid-1920s]. The sisters thought they were in the seventh heaven as before washing had to be on washboards and boiled in a large boiler, heated with coal and wood. Ironing was done with a flat iron and later we had electric irons and a small mangle.

"Student uniforms [for the girls] were changed to a one-piece sailor style with O.L.M. embroidered on the sleeve. Before this the boarders wore white middy blouses and a pleated blue or black skirt."

Unidentified students and nun on the grounds of Our Lady of Mercy Academy. The girl on the left is wearing the academy uniform. *Martin County Museum.*

Unidentified students with an academy nun. *Martin County Museum.*

Initially, to teach, sisters were required to have second grade, first grade, and permanent certificates from the state of Texas and would go to the University of Texas in Austin to obtain these. Sister Aloysius DuBronz explained that beginning in 1929, the sisters were required to have their Bachelor of Arts degree. Along with Sister Agnes McCabe, Sister Xavier Price, and Sister Ignatius Price, she attended West Texas College in Canyon, Texas. During this time, they stayed at Our Lady of Guadalupe in Amarillo, and someone had to drive the sisters 20 miles to Canyon for their classes. The sisters continued their studies at West Texas Teachers College for three years, but in 1932 the requisite was changed again, requiring sisters to receive their degrees from a Catholic college. The academy sisters transferred to Incarnate Word College in San Antonio to finish the requirements for their degrees.

When Sister Aloysius was attending classes in Canyon, she applied to the State of Texas for accreditation of Our Lady of Mercy Academy. A representative of the Texas education agency made a site visit. Her recommendations were to cover the windows on one side of one of the classrooms as "too much light was coming in." She also noted that the academy needed laboratory equipment. That was purchased at the cost of $350.00.

In her writings, Sister Aloysius provided the following inventory of what she described as a well-equipped library: novels, classics, histories, four sets of encyclopedias, periodicals, and magazines. After the site visit, the

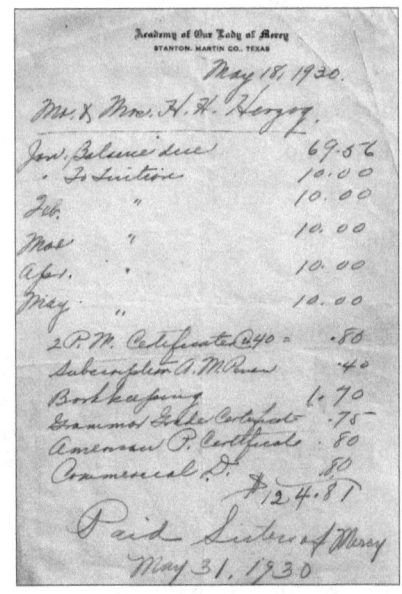

Invoice from Our Lady of Mercy Academy for tuition and supplies used by the Henry Herzog children. *Submitted by G. Walton*

school purchased a new set of maps in a case costing ten dollars and a new set of World's History for ninety dollars. "We began the process of affiliation and in a short time received Junior High credits in religion, Latin, algebra, world history, ancient history, English, biology, and general sciences. Each year one of the state supervisors visited the academy." Sister Aloysius noted, with satisfaction, "Now our school was comprised of several departments: High School, Commercial, Music and Art, Junior High, and Grammar Grades." At various times, a harmonica band performed, accompanied by Sister Aloysius on the piano. "The school had wonderful talents for debating, music, singing, and presenting three-act plays such as *Lady of the Lake*, *Red-Headed Step Child*, and *For the Love Mike*. In observance of St. Patrick's Day, the pupils gave a play, *My Wild Irish Rose*. The play was interspersed by the playing of piano duets and singing, which delighted the audience."

Sister Irma Multer, who attended the academy as a student from 1927 – 1930, later entered the Benedictine Order. The Sister's narrative, written in 1991, is a valuable, first-hand description of student life. As with many former students of the school, Sister Irma became a teacher. According to her obituary, she taught in public

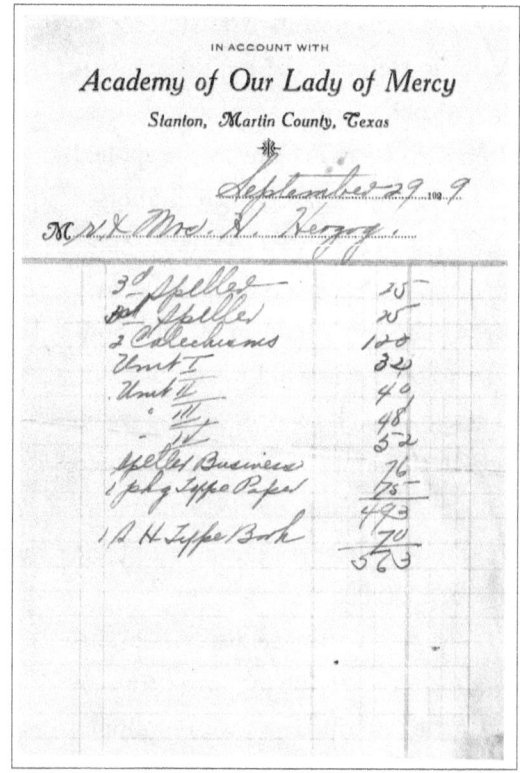

Invoice from Our Lady of Mercy Academy for supplies used by the Henry Herzog children. *Submitted by G. Walton*

schools in Texas and Florida and served as a principal of diocesan schools in Florida. Sister Irma Multer passed away in 2011. She was 97 years old.

Sister Irma also provided a drawing of the interior of the main building of the academy as she remembered it. Although the property surrounding the school was expansive, living quarters were tight when the student population was at its highest. Dorm space for boys and girls, the sisters' bedrooms, Mother Superior's office, sitting room, and bedroom were all on the second floor along with a library and classroom, an infirmary for the sisters, and a room where a sick student could be isolated.

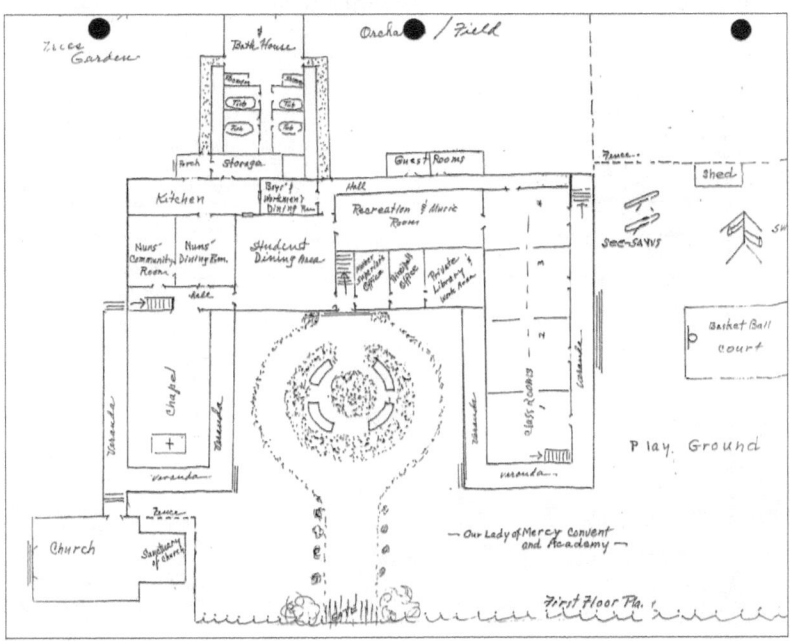

First Floor of main Academy building drawn from memory in 1991 by former student Sister Irma Multer. She attended the academy as a student from 1927 – 1930 and later entered the Benedictine Order. *Martin County Convent Foundation, Inc.*

Within five years, additional construction provided more dining space, parlors, a music room, a boys' dormitory, and a girls' dormitory, as well as more classrooms. At times, there were as many as seven pianos within the compound.

"It was a dry and hot day in August of 1927 when my mother, brother and I on a trip to New Mexico passed through Stanton. We heard of the old Carmelite church and convent and decided to visit this landmark; thus, we found Our Lady of Mercy Academy. The Sisters of Mercy welcomed us graciously, served us lemonade, and took us on a tour of the buildings. The academy, convent and church were an impressive sight on the vast barren plains of West Texas. The two storey [sic] structure of adobe brick and wood was built in an enlongated [sic] and inverted u-shape. A gravel driveway led from the street around a circular bed of flowers and trees.

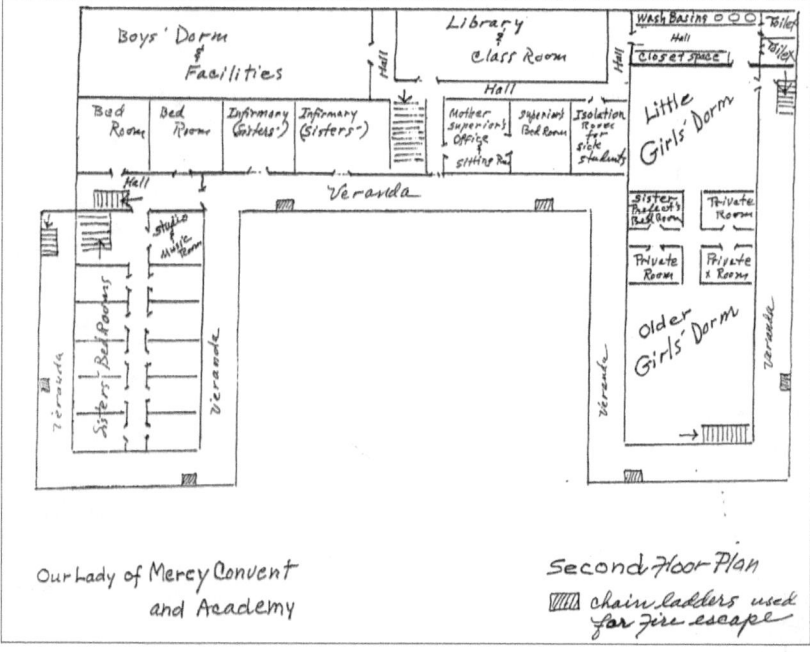

Second floor of main Academy building drawn from memory in 1991 by former student Sister Irma Multer, a student from 1927 – 1930. *Martin County Convent Foundation, Inc.*

"It was on our drive home that I decided to attend the academy. So, in September of 1927 I enrolled at Our Lady of Mercy academy as a sophomore in high school. I attended the academy for three terms from 1927 – 1930.

"Sister Aloysius DeBronz, Principal, and Mother Colomba Salmon, Superior of the Convent, helped to get me settled in. My parents arranged for a private room for me. Tuition, room, and board was $35.00 per month.

"My room was on the second floor next to the older girls' dormitory. The room was small, furnished with a bed, desk, chair and clothes closet. I enjoyed my privacy but often joined the girls in the dorm in their pranks – midnight snacks, pillow fights and climbing down the chain ladder fire escapes to the playground for a swing in the moonlight or just long sessions of girl talk. The cubicles in the dormitories were equipped with a bed and washstand. White curtains divided the cubicles. A nightlight was kept burning in the dorms and halls.

"Sister Perfect's room and three private rooms were located between the two dormitories. Certain house rules were strictly enforced. Discipline was firm but just.

"Most of the students, boys and girls, were boarders. They came from many of the neighboring towns: Odessa, Wink and Slaton. One of my classmates was the daughter of an Indian Chief from Oklahoma. Very few of the students at this time were of the Catholic persuasion.

"High academic standards were maintained at the academy. The teachers were highly qualified. In addition, the required high school curriculum, enrichment programs such as music, choral, art, penmanship, etiquette and social behavior were provided. Twice yearly the students presented a theatrical production; a pageant at Christmas and something classical in the spring semester. The one production I remember best was 'Little Women' most probably because I had the lead role.

"Sister Stanislaus Broderick was my piano teacher. Whenever I had performed unusually well at a session, Sister rewarded me by allowing me to play on the concert grand piano which stood in the recreation room. As a rule, students were not permitted to play on this instrument. I also took lessons in elocution from Sister Stanislaus. Sister conducted the class in a private studio on the second floor of the Convent building. It was a real privilege for me to walk through the hall into the Convent. Naturally I was curious to what I might see as I passed the Sisters' dining room and community room.

"The daily schedule began with Services (Mass) in the parish Church which was connected to the Convent verandah by a breeze-way of sorts. (Occasionally the older Catholic girls and boys privileged to attend Mass in the Convent Chapel.) After Mass we went to breakfast; and from there to our rooms to tidy up. We were expected to go out of doors for a bit of fresh air before classes began.

"Except for a fifteen-minute recess in mid-morning, classes continued until noon at which time dinner was served. After the meal we again had a short break for exercise in the fresh air. Classes ended at 3:00 o'clock. At this time, we were served a snack – an apple, a slice of water-melon (if in season) or a slice of bread and peanut butter. We were then required to spend an hour in outdoor activities. The older students played basketball or softball while the younger pupils played at various games. From 4:00 to 5:00 o'clock was 'Free Time' to read, browse in the library, practice piano or play. Study Hour began at 5:00 and lasted until supper at six o'clock. After supper we spent an hour in the recreation room singing, playing cards, checkers or just talking. Night prayers followed and then to bed. Lights out at 9:30 was strictly enforced.

"This was the routine from Monday through Friday. Saturday mornings were spent cleaning our rooms, learning to darn, mend and embroider or practice our penmanship. In the afternoon the older girls were permitted to go shopping, take long walks (chaperoned), play ball or spend time in the library. On rare occasions we went to Midland or Big Spring to enjoy a movie. Sundays were devoted to Church services in the early morning followed by an hour or so of letter writing to family and friends. The afternoon was free until five o'clock study hour.

"The schedule was quite structured; however, there were breaks in the routine for relaxation. Halloween was a time for a special party. The students dressed in costumes, bobbed for apples, played harmless pranks, etc. There were 'Taffy Pulls' and popcorn parties to enjoy. Once each semester we packed baskets of food and drove out to some ranch for a picnic and a cool swim in the pool."

Sisters of Mercy at Our Lady of Mercy Academy and Convent ca. 1936 (l to r) Sister Collazo, Sister Bronz, Sister Hoestetter, Sister Salmon, and Sister Rascon. *Martin County Convent Foundation, Inc.*

Another former student, Helen Dunn, wrote the following description, more than a half-century after she first arrived at the academy in 1936:

"As we drove through the wrought-iron gates that morning, I felt apprehensive. It wasn't as if I were afraid, because I had been away from my parents before, but through the eyes of a ten-year-old, the building appeared enormous, awesome, and rather interesting. It was 1936, late August. I was to spend nearly a year in the Sister of Mercy Convent at Stanton, Texas.

"The Convent was built in a horse-shoe shape with verandas running completely across the top and bottom floors. There were wooden railings along all of the verandas. From the top veranda you could see the whole town of Stanton and the surrounding area. [Ed. Note: Helen would soon learn that students were strongly discouraged from venturing out on the top floor veranda as the wooden flooring was deteriorating.] There were steps leading up to what I learned later was the main parlor. In the center of the driveway was a large bed of evergreens, shrubbery, and red cannas.

"We were greeted at the door by a nun, complete with black habit and hood, complimented by a square stiff white collar. A long rosary dangled from her waist. As she welcomed us, I noticed that she walked with a limp and wore, what I called a "funny shoe." She wore a nice smile, had chubby cheeks, and perched on her nose was a pair of gold-rimmed glasses. Her name was Sister Aloysius, and she was as formidable as the building itself. [Ed. Note: Sister Aloysius was the Principal of the academy at the time.]

"While my parents went into the office to take care of enrolling me, I was left to contemplate, speculate and examine a large room somber and dark with heavy drapes at the windows, religious pictures and some statutes. A huge black baby grand piano with enormous rounded legs stood in the center of the room.

It made our upright [piano] at home seem downright disgraceful!

"Tuition at this time was $30.00 a month plus $5 for piano lessons; however, I don't remember ever touching the keys on the beautiful baby grand. After making arrangements for my school year, my parents were ready to leave. With a lump in my throat and tears not far behind, I kissed them goodbye and the acrobatic butterflies in my stomach decided they were ready to settle in.

"My first night was restless. I laid there somewhat homesick and wondering what tomorrow would bring. I soon found out, for at six o'clock the bells began to ring so loud they curled your toes! We rose and made ourselves ready for morning mass in the Chapel.

"The nuns had been up much earlier preparing for the new day. When mass was over, we went to breakfast and then returned to our dorms to make beds and tidy up. My bedroom consisted of a bed, nightstand, and for privacy, a white curtain on a steel rod circled the small area. There were probably ten to twenty of these cubicles. Stairs at the end of this dormitory led to the classrooms below. Lavatories were located down a short hall and to the back of the building.

"During my entire stay [at the Convent] breakfast was the same with the exception of Easter. We were always served a large bowl of oatmeal, large slices of homemade bread and a cup of cocoa. The deviation from this meal at Easter was the addition of a fried egg. Since mutton was raised on the premises, we had it occasionally. I soon learned the meaning of 'eternal,' for the more you chewed this fine cuisine, the longer it lasted.

"After the evening meals, we helped with the dishes and then knelt to say rosary, before a short recreation time and then bed. At our recreational periods after supper, dishes, and rosary, we played games, sang songs, wrote letters or practiced piano or recitation.

"Saturday mornings were devoted to sewing, embroidery [sic], or mending along with piano practice. I worked the entire time I was attending the convent on an apron for my little sister, attempting to embroidery [sic] ducks on the front of it, but didn't finish.

"Classes at the convent began with Catechism, then the regular subjects. The nuns would spend much time with a student who was slow in order to keep them up with the class. They were very good instructors and fortunately, I made mostly As, with a few Bs.

"My class teacher was Sister Florence and she was from Ireland. She was not immune to playing kickball with us or joining in on our games. She was kind, not too tall, and slim. I can still see her long black skirt flying and her equally long rosary jangling as she ran.

"The bath houses were located behind the convent, which also served as the laundry. We usually bathed on Saturday and this was too often for me as during the week, spiders set up housekeeping in the bottom of the tub and they had to be done away with before we could take our baths.

"Most of the girls and boys attending this convent were from neighboring towns, whose parents wished them to be educated in the Catholic faith. The closest Catholic school would have been Loretto Academy in El Paso or one in Fort Worth or Dallas. There were also 'day' students' who attended from Stanton.

"We were allowed to go home for the weekend every two or three weeks or when our parents could come for us. Sometimes my parents would come on Sunday for mass and we would drive to Big Spring for dinner and to see a movie. Sometimes they could not come at all and it was so lonesome when everyone else gone, but the sisters sensed this and would pay us attention, and the weekend would pass quicker.

"The church we attended on Sundays and most Catholic holidays was located across the street from the convent. This church was called St. Joseph and at the time of attendance, the pastor was Rev. E.M. Chevrier, A.M. I made my 'solemn' Communion in this church."

Chapter 10
A Look Back at Learning

It is impossible to accurately assess the far-reaching influence of the Sisters of Mercy in their service at Our Lady of Mercy Academy and Convent. Most accounts credit the academy with providing a high-level educational experience for over 3,000 students during its operating years from 1894 – 1938.

An undated article found in the Catholic Archives of Texas lists "some of the most useful citizens in the Stanton Community" who received their elementary education at Our Lady of Mercy Academy: Jim Tom, cashier of the First National Bank of Stanton; Paul Daily, a successful teacher in New York City; and Paul Konz, now pursuing his studies for his PhD degree. But possibly more important than these are the many mothers of the Stanton community who received their early training there, and now are counted among the most faithful patrons of the institution."

Perhaps the earliest available record of an academy student is of Delia Cecilia (Scholz) Schwarzenbach who, according to her son, John F. Schwarzenbach, came to the colony from Germany in 1881 with her parents Theodor and Anna Scholz when she was three years old. She attended Our

Lady of Mercy Academy when she was 11. The young woman married Reynold Schwarzenbach, a locomotive engineer and the couple had six children. Delia passed away March 30, 1958 and is buried in the Mount Olive Cemetery, Big Spring, Texas.

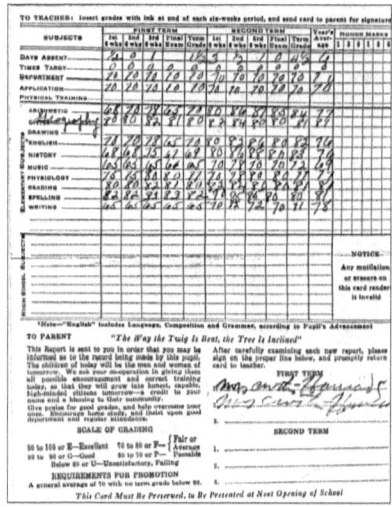

Class grades of ten-year-old Andrew Hancock, student at the Academy 1936 - 37. *Martin County Convent Foundation, Inc.*

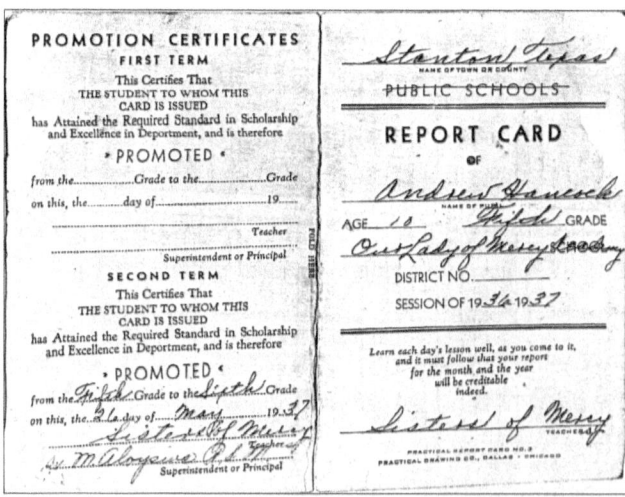

Report card of ten-year-old Andrew Hancock, student at the Academy 1936 - 37. *Martin County Convent Foundation, Inc.*

Lena Lynelle (Hasey) Ringener provided her family's connection to the convent: "After the death of my grandmother, Mary Newman Bell in 1903, the four children went to live at the convent – Minnie Evelyn (my mother), Nellie May, Edgar Edward, and Mabel." Their father, George Lawrence Bell, helped with the first electric and telephone lines from Big Spring to Stanton. The children stayed at the convent about two months when Minnie Evelyn was 11 years old; Nellie May was eight; Edgar Edward, who was deaf, was six years old; Mabel was five. Minnie Evelyn talked very little about her time at the convent, but did explain [to her daughter] that she helped take care of the other three children, especially Mabel, who cried most of the time. Minnie Evelyn described the nuns as "real sweet to all of them, but I was cold most of the time."

Mamie Connell (right) in her Our Lady of Mercy Academy uniform with unidentified student. *Martin County Museum.*

Charles Walker Glascock and Mary Losch, an immigrant from Katzenhirn, Mindelau, Germany were married on July 21, 1897 in Marienfeld. The couple were parents to six children: Florence Theresa, William Vance, Raymond Leon, Truman Lee, John Wesley Ashford, and Charlene Elizabeth. All of the Glascock children attended school at the convent between 1907 – 1918. Florence Theresa's daughter, Margaret, shared some family memories: "The nuns would not allow Florence to wear bangs, telling her that her hair must be pulled back 'so we can see your forehead.' Charlene, the youngest child, was left-handed and she vividly remembered 'the sting of the ruler training her to write the right way…right-handed.' She did learn to write with her right hand, but 'all else was done left-handed.'"

Although many of the children who came to the academy were there for an education, the situation was often more imperative. When a mother died, she usually left a husband with young children and no one to help. A rancher or farmer who worked sunup to sundown simply could not handle a young family alone. In these circumstances, the structured, devoted care provided by the Sisters of Mercy had a lifelong impact on the children who lived and learned at the convent.

The Sisters of Mercy cared for three generations of the Smythe/Scott family: Peter and Anna Smythe; their daughter, Nannie (Smythe) Scott; and Nannie's two children, Dollie and Alvin. This is but one example of the impact the nuns had on the residents of this outlying area, providing education, spiritual guidance, and, often, a safe haven.

Dollie Scott was four years old and her brother, Alvin, was two when they came to Our Lady of Mercy Academy. Their father, T.P. Scott, was a rancher in Martin County, and their mother, Nannie, had died of a long-term respiratory illness. The father was familiar with the Sisters of Mercy Academy because his wife attended the school when she was young, graduating in June of 1888, one month before she and T.P. married.

This weathered, heart-broken man delivered his two young children to the nuns knowing they would be in good hands. Ten years would pass before Mr. Scott remarried and returned to the convent to take his children home. Except now, there was only his daughter. His son, Alvin, died at the convent in 1903 at the age of eight. The cause of young Alvin's death is unknown.

Dollie wrote this letter to her father on Christmas Day, 1898. She was five and a half years old.

"Dear Papa, the best day of all the year has come and I wish you a Very Merry Christmas and a Happy New Year. I would like you to

come and see me. Old Santa Claus will be here and Sister says he will have some thing nice for your little girl; so, please come and we will have such a good time.
From your loving little Dollie Scott"

Two years later, Dollie wrote this letter to her father:

"Dear Papa, I am well and growing so big I fear you will not know me next time you come to see me. We had a candy party the other day. The large girls cooked it and we little ones ate it. I practice on the piano every day and go to school too. Give my love to Grandpa and Grandma Peter and much love and a kiss to you from your little girl. Dollie Scott"

Students at Our Lady of Mercy Academy ca. 1898. Dollie Scott, five and a half years old, is pictured in the front holding her doll. *Martin County Museum.*

Years later, the Sisters of Mercy cared for Dollie's grandparents, Peter and Anna Smythe. After Anna passed away, the nuns provided Peter, who suffered from dementia, a room at the convent until his death ten years later. Peter, Anna, Nannie, and Alvin are all buried in St. Joseph Cemetery.

At the time of Dollie's grandfather, Peter Smythe's, death in 1919, *The Odessa Herald*, published the following article:

"A letter to The Herald from the Sisters of Mercy at Stanton, brings news of the death, in the home which these good women had provided for him and in which they had tenderly cared for him for the past ten years, on the 16th ultimo, of Peter Smythe, a former resident of Odessa, and familiarly known to the former residents of this place as "Uncle Peter.

"'He had no diseases,' writes the sisters, 'but his mind was shattered. He died of old age and was laid to rest here in our cemetery.' The wife of Peter Smythe preceded him by many years to the Better Land, while even before this, the only child that had blessed their long union, Mrs. Nannie Scott, had passed away. Thus, the old man had been alone for many years, during which time he was cared for by the Sisters of the Academy of Our Lady of Mercy at Stanton.

"For many years Uncle Peter was a familiar figure in Odessa and had a powerful influence over its affairs. After the organization of Ector county, he was, for many years, a sort of general deputy to all of the county officers, being by far the best educated man in the county."

Other students attended the academy for other practical, but less dire reasons. Lauryn Westerman Pritchett attended the school at Stanton in 1909 when she was 10 years old. Lauryn lived with her family in Big Spring, Texas, but that year the schools in her hometown were full. Her father took Lauryn and her sister to the academy for the school year.

Vergie Mae (Henson) Atchison attended the academy in 1910 and again in 1920. Vergie began school in the second grade in 1909 in the "old jail house [in Stanton]. My books kept being stolen so [I was] sent to the convent." After graduating from high school elsewhere, Vergie returned to the school in 1920 to take a business course. "We had to take a blindfold test once a week in typing. The sisters made me nervous. The girls that boarded there dressed alike in white blouses and navy blue, pleated skirts." Other girls who attended the school with Vergie in 1920 were: Edith Cooper, Mary Morgan, Ida (Henson) Kennady, Ada (Henson) Hopkins, May (Douglas) Henson, Ila (Henson) Hammit, Villia Tom Wilkerson, Alma Herzog, and Cecilia Herzog.

Mother Superior Angela Hoestetter, served at Our Lady of Mercy Academy and Convent 1895 – 1921. Date of photo unknown. *Martin County Convent Foundation, Inc.*

During the time that Sister Angela Hoestetter was Mother Superior of the academy, 1913 – 1921, she tried to adhere to a policy of accepting one "charity" student for every four students who could pay a boarding tuition. In one circumstance, a man came to the convent one night with small unkempt children. His wife was on the verge of death from consumption, and he wanted to take her to a hospital. Sister Angela Hoestetter took the children in for what she thought would be a short stay. She never heard from the man again. Sister Angela allowed the children to stay at the academy, educated them, and kept in touch with each of them until the time of her death.

Another father turned to the Sisters of Mercy to help with his six young children after his wife died. George Clinton Cauble was a rancher near Big Spring, Texas where he lived with his wife, Mollie. In a brief, handwritten family history, George's granddaughter, Ola Ruth Edens, states that in the early 1900s, George "lost his wife when his 6 children – Willie, Ovie Birdie, Edna, Leatha, George Jr., and Samuel – were very young. They were put in the Catholic Convent for their education." In 1912, Ola Ruth, daughter of Ovie Birdie, also attended the convent school for three years while her parents were working on the McDowell Ranch in Central Texas Hill Country. "The convent was very nice with lots of rooms and lots of students," Ola Ruth wrote. "It was a very pretty building. The family all took music and graduated in music. The Sisters of Mercy served lots of roast beef and potatoes. I learned to play the piano and I learned the rosary."

In the mid-1980s, the Stanton Jaycees attempted to purchase the convent property. A previous student, Margaret Lupton, sent a letter to the Jaycees in support of their efforts: "I spent many happy years at the convent, first when Mother Angela was in charge [1913 – 1921] and again during my junior high-school year. It was a fine school and I attribute much of my success in life to it. I also taught at the school after finishing my education in Ft. Worth. Cannot remember the name of the nun in charge at that time. I certainly wish you well…it was a wonderful old building and I would love to see it preserved. Sincerely, Peg Brandt (formerly Margaret Lupton), El Cajon, California.

Mabel (Sherman) Curry began her education in a one-room schoolhouse at Sawyer Flat, approximately 30 miles east of Seminole, Texas in Gaines County. However, that school only taught students through the eighth grade and Mabel enrolled at the academy to complete her education.

Her grandson and author of the *Hank the Cowdog* book series, John Erickson, described the convent school in an article published in *Texas Highways* as "the only school of its caliber for the sparse but growing population between Fort Worth and El Paso. By the time Grandmother Curry attended Mercy Academy, it boasted an enrollment of 100, mostly daughters of ranchers from Big Spring, Midland, Odessa, San Angelo, Menard, Lubbock, and Post. They studied literature, Latin, rhetoric, needlework, and music. If Grandmother exemplified what the sisters turned out at Mercy Academy, they were excellent teachers."

Mabel is an example of many non-Catholic children who attended the academy. Her family was part of a contingency of Quakers who established the town of Estacado in Crosby County. The Sherman family later moved to Gaines County.

Ten-year-old Elizabeth (Lupton) Owen, along with her brother and three sisters attended the academy 1918 – 1920. Throughout her time in Stanton, Elizabeth made brief, daily entries in her diary about studying, attending Mass, and helping with chores. She also wrote about the celebration of holidays such as May Day and Arbor Day as well as usual major holidays. Letters from home and occasional visits from her mother were noteworthy. Upon arrival at the school in January, she wrote that "Sister Evangelist vaccinated us all. Didn't hurt very much, but I caught cold in mine and surely did suffer."

Occasionally, the spunky young girl with red hair clashed with the sisters. "Just came in from recess and as I was putting up my tatting, Sister Aloysius took it away from me. I don't like her at all and won't study either until she gives it back to me. Answered Sister Aloysius back I am sorry to say and Sister Dillon gave me the hardest whipping."

A few weeks later, the incident apparently forgotten, Elizabeth writes: "Sister Aloysius is going to quit the girls' house – that was one dear teacher I hate to lose."

Another entry: "Sister Augustine will not let us play hop-scotch any more as it wears out our shoes."

Although Elizabeth wrote in her diary that she planned to graduate from Our Lady of Mercy Academy and "be a sister," her family moved to California and she graduated from San Diego High School instead.

Elizabeth continued her education at San Diego Teachers College, West Texas State College, New Mexico State College and Texas Technological College and started her teaching career in 1924. Elizabeth retired after 53 years in the classroom. The final two decades of her career she taught second grade at Christ the King Cathedral School in Lubbock, Texas. Elizabeth died July 8, 2011. She was 104 years old.

Emma Jean (Emmagene Davis) York and her brothers, William and Mark Davis, lived at the academy between the years of 1918 and 1921. "My brother William worked with Mr. Koonz helping milk the cows and take care of the chickens. He would also get the mail at the post office in Stanton and deliver it to the Mother Superior. I remember Sister Delores at the convent, but she left the order while we were there. I worked some in the girls' dormitory and in the dining room." Mark was too young to work, but because their mother couldn't pay tuition for her children, William and Emmagene performed tasks for the sisters. "Our mother, Mattie Lee Davis, was a widow and worked at a Catholic hospital in Big Spring, Texas. She would ride the train to Stanton to see us about once a month. The sisters were very good to us. The children who were not Catholic went to church; the Catholics went to mass." The flu epidemic occurred while the Davis children lived at the Convent. "The sisters took care of everyone even though some of them were sick, too." Emmagene remembers when her brother Mark and another young boy stashed some eggs and built a fire in a bucket to boil them. "The bucket turned over and burned Mark's leg. The sisters doctored him and took care of him, but didn't punish him."

Jim McGinnis was a full-time boarder at the school from the spring of 1922 through the fall of 1927. "Mother Berchmans was there when I was a student. She would go out walking in the pasture after Mass with us and we would have to hold the barbed wire fence apart for her to clamber through, rosaries and all. She was a good sport. We would climb up the wheel tower of the windmill by the kitchen, and slide down the pipe that enclosed the sucker rods. The wheel tower was high – about 65 feet, and the pipe was 50 feet high. We did this in plain view of the sisters, who never made us stop. I remember a very young, pretty nun – Sister Mary Michael – who was in charge of the boys who lived in the boys' dorm. She was responsible for teaching me the Latin responses so I could serve as altar boy."

Sister Ruth Mercedes Jefferies entered Our Lady of Mercy Academy and Convent in 1928. She attended the academy as a student 1924-26. *Martin County Convent Foundation, Inc.*

Ruth Jeffries attended Our Lady of Mercy Academy from 1924 – 1926 and entered the Mercy convent as Sister Mercedes in 1928. She later served over 50 years at Mercy Hospital in Slaton, Texas. Her younger sister, Sophie (Jeffries) White recalls visiting the convent as a young child, "I remember the stairway in the front entrance. It had red carpet and it looked like it went all the way to heaven! The church looked huge to me. It seemed as though the altar almost touched the ceiling. It was Easter time and the altar was loaded with Easter lilies. Such a wonderful scent. Today when I smell Easter lilies it smells like the convent at Stanton."

Sophie, Ruth's sister, attended tenth grade at the academy from September, 1937 to May, 1938. "The porches were great to get out of the sun. There were no air conditioners then. But it was very cold in the winter as it was hard to heat a building with such high ceilings. The nuns put a basket full of Easter eggs by my bed for me to find Easter morning. I was so homesick, from September to Thanksgiving I thought that if I could ever get home, I would never leave. I went home at Thanksgiving with all intentions of staying. But when I got home it was different. All of my friends were scattered and my best friend had married. And, my boyfriend had found another girl! When the holidays were over, I went back to the convent." Sophie was an "A" student in classes that included Christian Doctrine, Sacred History, Geometry, English, U.S. History, Biology, Deportment, and Application.

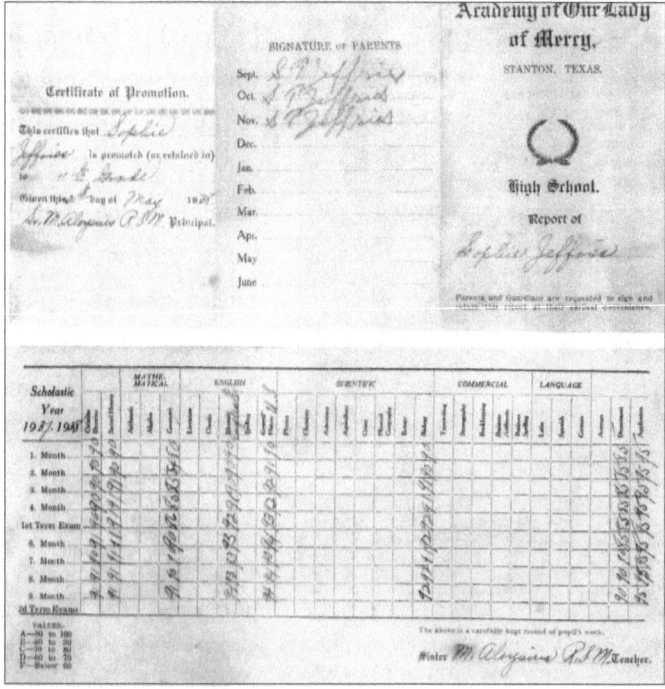

Report card of Sophie Jefferies who attended the Academy from September, 1937 to May, 1938. *Martin County Convent Foundation, Inc.*

In an interview for the *Big Spring Herald* in 1993, Winnie Connell recalled her time at the academy. She attended her senior year in 1933 as a boarding student. "My fondest memories of this school are the times we shared together. There really weren't enough students the same age to have a great deal of activities, but we would have big dances up in the attic and those were always fun. This was a good school."

Jack H. Lewis responded to a request from the Martin County Convent Foundation with his memories of the time he was at the Our Lady of Mercy boarding school from 1928 – 1930:

"Most of my childhood years were spent, until the age of 9, in boarding homes and home for boys. My mother, Maurine Beauchamp, had placed me in the Convent when I was four years old. I recall walking with her from a car to a building that seemed far away. The doors were very large and once inside sisters met us at the door. We went to a room where my mother talked to one of them. In some way I knew I would be staying here.

"Later I remember a sister dressing me and telling me we were going to a funeral. We were not gone very long so it must have been close by. I thought it may have been one of the sisters that passed away although there is no remembrance of the funeral, only the sisters, priest and casket.

"There were swings next to the building. One of the wooden seats had cut my forehead and three stitches were taken to close the cut. I believe it was the summer of 1930 when my grandparents had taken me from the Convent and sending [sic] me to my mother in Los Angeles, California."

Although he doesn't recall his actual learning experience at the academy, Jack is certain the sisters "must have taught me something for I received a certificate for writing and an exceptionally good grade for reading in the first grade at my Los Angeles school."

Marcelle (Sally) McAnalley Rosenthal and her brother, Bill H. McAnalley attended the school from September, 1935 to May, 1936. Sally was in the fourth grade and Bill in the fifth. Sally contacted the Martin County Convent Foundation in 1991 seeking records of past students. "We left under a request due to facts of a strict, broken rule."

Young Nick Sanchez who lived in Stanton, attended the academy three years in the mid-1930s. "I used to run in the corridors when we got a break. I liked to get stars for learning my prayers."

Our Lady of Mercy Academy held annual commencement exercises to recognize students who were graduating and to celebrate the end of the school year. The June 1913 ceremony was typical of these celebrations. The opening address was given by Miss Josephine Tubbs. An instrumental duet was offered by Miss Helen Dinwadde and Miss Agnes Phelps, followed by a recitation by Master Clifford Robertson who was ably assisted by the Junior Boys class. *The Stanton Reporter* further reported that the flower song by Miss Alma Richards assisted by the intermediate girls was splendid. An essay by Miss Laura Hancock entitled, "Not for School but for Life We Learn," was well rendered.

Handwritten entries in Angela Tom's keepsake book in 1916 and 1917 provide understanding of a teenage girl's life while she was attending the academy. A partial list of the girls who were at the school with Angela during this time includes: Catherine Clarke, Dorothy Jenkins, Eddie Stevenson, Lelia Tom, Mamie Robertson, Iva Sherrill, Mary Caroline, Ethel Cross, and Katherine Tinnin.

Two entries on the "Jokes and Frolics" page in the book are amusing descriptions of students who broke some of the academy rules:

> "Quaint yet ridiculous is the picture that looms up before our visions when we recall the very sandstorming day when Jennie, Clyde, Mary Fletcher, Jane Lee and Angela were stationed on East Porch to muse awhile in punishment for talking in ranks at noon. To a traveller [sic] and stranger we might present the aspect of 5 black crows all seated on a bench enjoying the

benefits of the sand. Some joy we had too, though our lessons were failures.

"Dance did I hear someone say? No not for Villa, Carrie and Ruth. Jane Lee and I will ever remember the night those three slipped off and went to a dance at Hotel Stanton. O, but we were all rather uneasy."

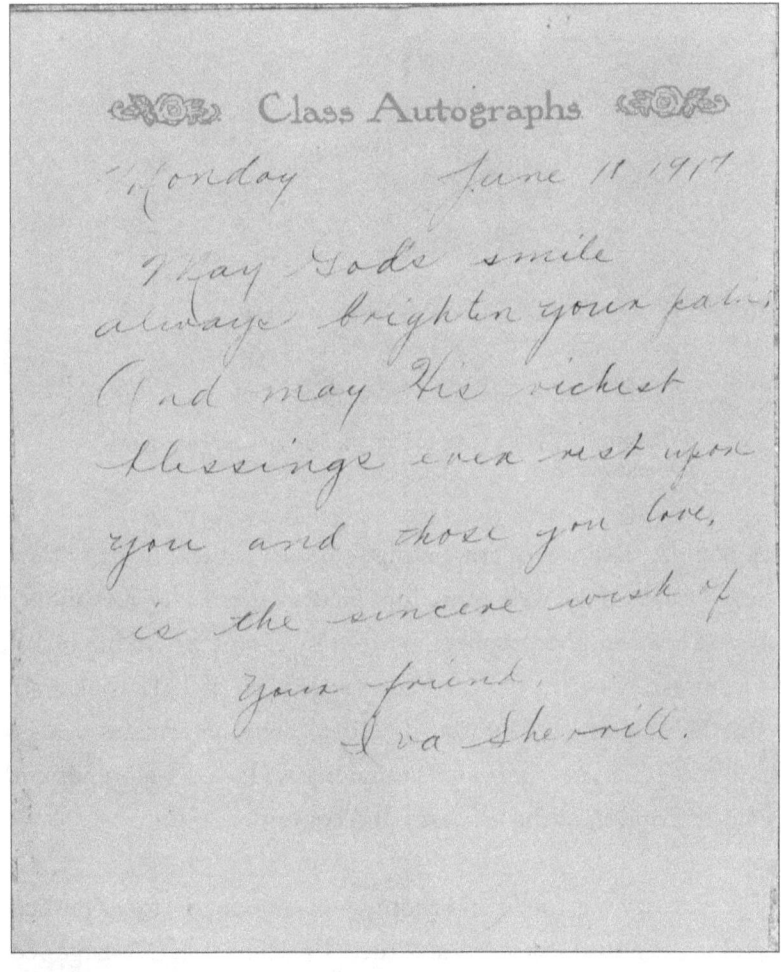

Class autograph written by Iva Sherrill to Angela Tom for Angela's "memory book." The girls were seniors at the academy in 1917. *Martin County Convent Foundation, Inc.*

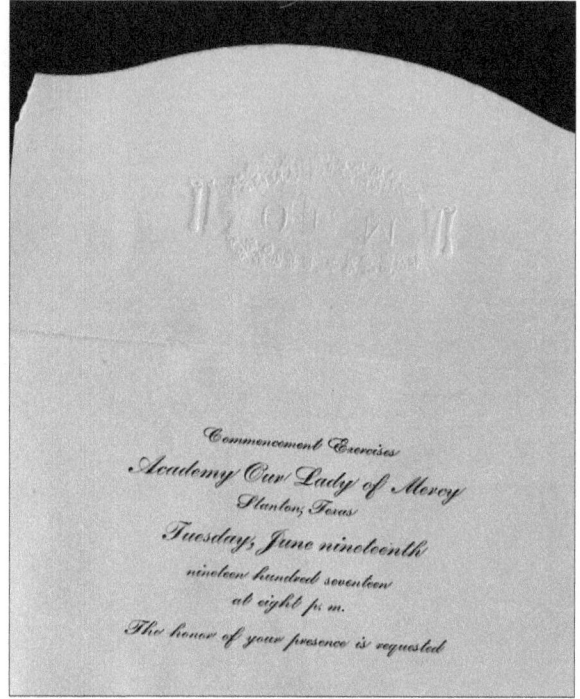

Class of 1917 graduation invitation. *Martin County Convent Foundation, Inc.*

A popular tradition of graduating seniors was the writing of the class prophecy. Usually these were humorous pieces with inside jokes about class members. However, the prophecy written by Dorothy Jenkins in Angela Tom's keepsake book for the academy senior class of 1917 took a serious turn. In the beginning, Dorothy described some classmates years after graduation as brides, teachers and a missionary. However, she ends with an ominous description of the academy and convent:

"The pathway was rough and thorny, and large sharp stones pushed up along the road. So worn and tired I reached a gate, a large red gate. So opening it and passing up a long walk I beheld – to my dismay – a heap of ashes – stones, and brick – nothing remained (for

I knew it was my loved home, my convent), save the corner stone of the church where once we had all gone so happy and peaceful to pray. Nothing was left now so I fell upon the stone and wept.

"Someone was shaking me and saying…'The prayer bell has rung and we are waiting on you.' I rubbed my eyes and sat up. The moon was shining in the classroom window and it was late. So, reluctantly I went upstairs thinking after all it was only a dream, but who knows? It may be true."

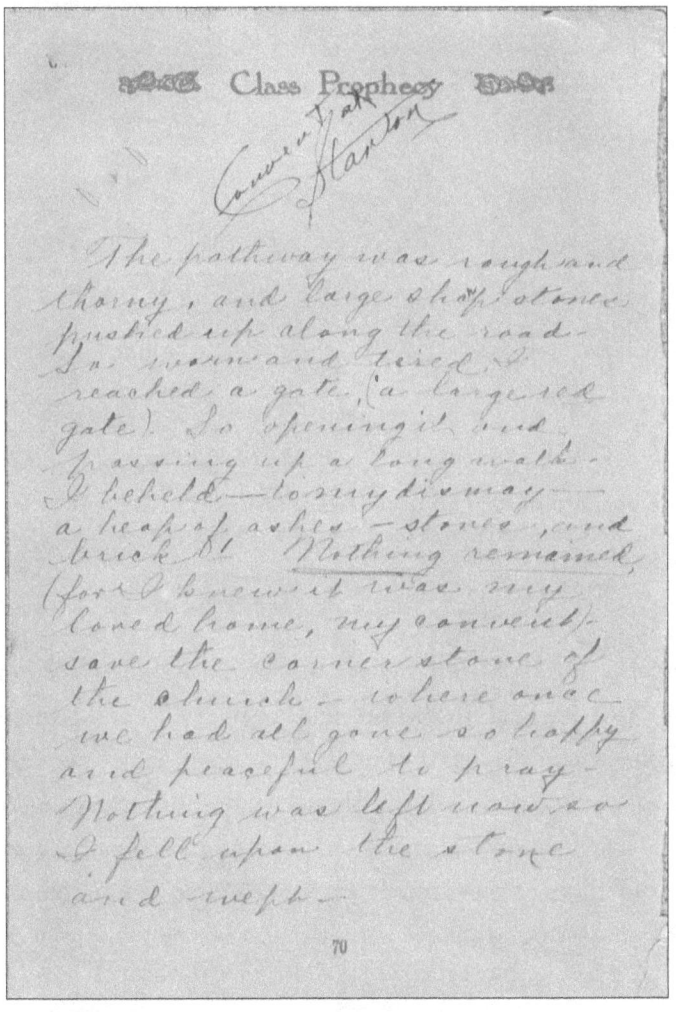

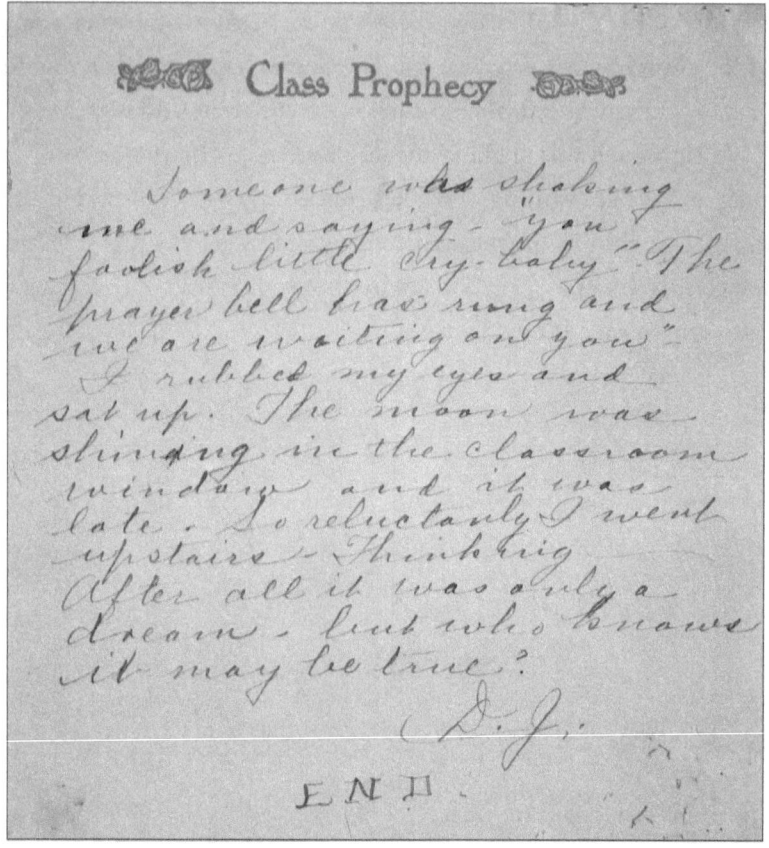

Class Prophecy predicting the destruction of Our Lady of Mercy Academy and Convent written in 1917 by student Dorothy Jenkins. *Martin County Convent Foundation, Inc.*

Dorothy Jenkins' class prophecy was indeed predictive. Many of her classmates married and Eddie Stevenson spent her adult life teaching. Angela Tom entered the convent in 1922 and as a Mary Knoll Sister, went to Korea as a missionary in 1927. The teenager's unsettling description of a ravaged convent in the dream sequence of the 1917 prophecy would also be a true foretelling of the future. Two decades later, in a matter of minutes, a force majeure would leave the academy and convent compound in ruin.

Chapter 11
The Academy in Ruin

Almost 20 years after coming to the academy at Stanton, at the age of 68, Mother Superior Berchmans Kast relinquished her responsibilities as Superior of the Convent to her protégé, Sister Mary Angela Hoestetter. Mother Berchmans continued to live at the convent for eight years. Leading up to her decision to step down, a delegate of the bishop submitted written reports in 1911 and again in 1912, indicating discontent within the convent with several sisters speaking of their dissatisfaction with the government of the community. The recommendation to remedy the situation was to replace Mother Superior. The bishop installed Sister Angela as Mother Superior in 1913, and she served in that capacity until 1921.

In her writings, Kathleen O'Brien, R.S.M. describes Mother Berchmans at this time as fearing that she would die of a broken heart if she did not find some way to be useful. "I am in the best of health (except for my broken heart)," she told Bishop Shaw in a November 18, 1912 letter, "and if Your lordship will give me several hundred Mexicans to care for I…would, I know give satisfaction and feel young and happy once more…"

Sister Angela Hoestetter, who originally came to Stanton to work alongside Mother Berchmans, was very distressed and pained with the situation and wrote the bishop:

"Your Lordship must be aware of the fact that Mother M. Berchmans has been unable to act for years past. There is much that may be said; but as matters are so complex it may be best to say as little as possible. Permit me to be as brief as possible, as I am heart-broken over existing deplorable conditions. Why we have been left in such a critical state for so many years is beyond comprehension. The only consolation was the firm belief that the Almighty had a purpose in it, and that He would reveal it in His own good time. In this isolated place, no advice was to be had; what was done for the best proved the worst. How we have held together is a miracle unless, as before quoted, the Almighty has a purpose in it."

In 1921, the founder of Our Lady of Mercy Academy and Convent, Mother Mary Berchmans Kast, aged 77, moved to Slaton, Texas, to open St. Joseph School. In 1939 the Slaton parish honored Mother Berchmans with a general communion and solemn high mass to celebrate the 75th anniversary of her entrance into religious service. St. Joseph parish school continued operating until May 2017.

Just before her 95th birthday, Mother Berchmans died peacefully in Mercy Hospital in Slaton on the Feast of the Immaculate Conception, December 8, 1939. She is buried in Englewood Cemetery in Slaton.

Sister Mary Stanislaus Broderick, who was at the academy from 1913 until it closed in 1938, taught elementary grades and music, served as Mistress of Novices and replaced Mother Berchmans as Superior of the Convent 1921 – 28. Sister Stanislaus was born in Ireland and educated in New York. She was professed in 1884 in San Patricio, Texas. Before coming to the academy, her service focused on the education of youth in various mission fields of the Sisters of Mercy in south and west Texas.

Sister Mary Stanislaus Broderick who served at Our Lady of Mercy Academy and Convent from 1913 until it closed in 1938. She was Mother Superior 1921 - 28. *Martin County Museum.*

A letter written in 1972 by Sister Mary Xavier Price, who came to Stanton from Ireland in 1912 and served at the academy until 1925, described Sister Stanislaus Broderick as "a good and holy soul, which was our impression. She taught classes, also piano, but she lacked the gifts, talents, personality and business ability of Mother Mary Angela. She was very jealous of any novice the sisters might merit or receive. She was not much for work but commanded and supervised the sisters to accomplish things. She had no understanding of purchasing or providing needs for the sisters. Although she was helpless, she was prayerful and kept the sisters long moments on their knees with special prayers."

Sister Xavier Price presumed that the personality and harsh leadership of Mother Stanislaus caused unhappiness among the sisters. "I believe that the sisters who could not take it did what they did, many of them could not go along with the new administration and withdrew to join their former superior [in forming the Foundation in Raton, New Mexico]. It is good to remember here that this is the opinion and observation of only one of the Sisters of Mercy who served at the Academy and we are not privy to the opinion of others regarding the leadership of Mother Stanislaus."

Spending most of her religious life teaching in various schools, Sister Xavier Price retired in May 1970 at the age of 78. After retirement, she was Sacristan at Convent of Mercy in Slaton, Texas, and continued teaching. She wrote, "Convent duties take most of my time. I teach two Spanish classes at St. Joseph's School. I also train the altar boys in the parish church so I'm not retired from work. We (the retired) spend extra time in prayer – prayers for the success of the Institute, for all who ask our prayers, etc. etc."

Sister Xavier wrote fondly of Mother Berchmans, who had recruited her to come to Stanton. "She retired in 1913. She was not young then, but she did her utmost to instill in us the spirit of service. She remained a good religious and a model of poverty, spending most of her late years in the chapel."

A report from the Catholic Diocese of Amarillo stated that "as the number of students increased at the academy in Stanton, junior high and high school subjects were added. In 1925 the academy received an accredited rating as a junior high school. A commercial course was conducted, and departments of music, arts, and home economics were included in the school curriculum."

The academy compound developed into a social center where folks from the far-flung corners of the area could gather in Stanton for significant religious events and special celebrations. The students performed plays and musical programs for parents and the community.

An article in the *Big Spring Daily Herald* in April of 1937 describes a special birthday celebration for a young boy:

"Dallas Childers, Jr., was honored guest at a party given in Our Lady of Mercy Academy in Stanton Saturday afternoon when his mother arranged the affair to celebrate his birthday anniversary. Although the Childers reside in Forsan, the entertainment was held at the academy where the sister of the honored guest is attending school.

"The dining table was centered with a large white birthday cake topped with five lighted candles, and slices of it were served with ice cream of four attractive colors. Twelve children were served that included the honored guest's two sisters, Nell and Millicent Anne.

"The group played a number of games and later posed for pictures. Afterward they were entertained by Mrs. Childers who played violin selections. Assisting in the hospitalities were Miss Mildred Newell of this city and Sister Aloysius and Sister Mary Lourdes of the academy."

Sister Mary Lourdes Barron at Our Lady of Mercy Academy and Convent. *Martin County Convent Foundation, Inc.*

The young boy's sister, Valdeva Nell Childers, celebrated her 13th birthday the next month. The *Big Spring Daily Herald* also reported that event. It isn't clear if the mention of a farewell for departing students refers to the end of the school year or alludes to the plans to close the academy permanently.

> "The dining hall of Our Lady of Mercy Academy in Stanton was beautifully decorated with bouquets of roses and other spring flowers Sunday afternoon when Valdeva Nell Childers, daughter of Mr. and Mrs. Dallas Childers of this city, celebrated her 13th birthday anniversary with a party at the academy where she is a student. The party also served as a sort of farewell affair for the pupils who will be leaving the convent.
>
> "After many games the children gathered about the long dining table where they were served refreshments. The birthday cake was decorated in pink and white and was topped with pink candles held in green holders.
>
> "Academy students attending were Marjorie Green, Mary Ann Decklemann, Iria Anderson, Carmen Vasquez, Kenneth Lewis, Colleen Hoge, Rita McMillan, Angela Schell, Loretta Schell, Dixie Evans, Temple Perkins, O'Brien Lewis, Marshall Lewis, Charles Tom and Sister Mary Aloysius, Sister Mary Lourdes and Sister Mary Stanislaus. Accompanying Mrs. Childers from here were her children, Dallas, Jr., and Millicent Ann, and Misses Violet Newell and Elizabeth Carruthers."

Funding for the Academy of Our Lady of Mercy primarily came from the proceeds of board and tuition charges. Many of the students from farm and ranch families, and during the years of diminished farm income in the area, many boarders were kept at a reduced rate. Some could not pay any amount. Another factor that caused a decline in enrollment was a corresponding decline in the Catholic population in the area. The organization of more local public schools and the establishment of more private schools throughout Texas and the United States also negatively affected the enrollment and financial stability of the academy. However, despite the ups and downs of enrollment and corresponding income, Our Lady of Mercy Academy maintained its high standards and excellent reputation for more than four decades.

Main entrance to Our Lady of Mercy Academy and Convent compound, 1935. *Martin County Foundation, Inc.*

The 1938 faculty, the last to serve at the academy, according to a report written by Mother Superior DuBronz, was: Sister Aloysius DuBronz, High School; Sister Agnes McCabe, Sister Rudolpha, and Sister Lourdes Barron, Grammar School Grades; Sister Stanislaus Broderick, Music; Sister Reto and Sister Josephine Bourgeois, various other responsibilities.

The June 17, 1938 edition of the *Stanton Reporter* featured this front-page headline:

Small Twister Cuts Gash Through Town Doing about $30,000 Worth of Damage

Mother Superior's report within the article stated that "the Catholic convent suffered the most damage. Three windmills were flattened to the ground, the roof on the north side of the convent building torn off, church wrenched badly, and roof on the south side of the priest's home lifted off."

The following is another description of the events of June 11, 1938, from *A History of the Convent and Academy of Our Lady of Mercy*, compiled by Franchelle Moore in 1963:

"On June 11, eight sisters and one boarder were in the building when, after a very sultry afternoon, ominous clouds began to form in the southwest. About 6 o'clock, the wind rose and soon consumed the proportions of a tornado, striking the convent and academy buildings with full force. In a few moments, the laundry, barns, and other out-buildings collapsed; the windmills toppled over in masses of twisted steel, one crashing into the roof of the north portions of the convent.

"Next the roof of the center building became detached, and a large part of it was blown away; bits of wreckage from other structures were flying through the dust-laden air. After the storm had subsided, the rain began to fall in torrents, pouring into the girls' dormitory. The old convent building withstood the fury of the wind, and, although suffering considerable damage, still was habitable.

"Almost everything of value was disposed of, including the partly demolished center building; and the sisters left to work in other locations. Several of the sisters transferred to Mercy Hospital in Slaton, Texas."

Ten-year-old Virginia (Ragland) Urey was the only student at the convent when the devastating tornado hit. Her family lived in El Paso, and her parents sent her to the convent for school in 1937. "I have a plethora of memories of those two years of my life. I had attended the school in the winter, living in the dorm. In the summertime, I had to stay there alone with the Sisters while the other children went home."

On the day of the tornado, Virginia was in the kitchen with several Sisters washing dishes, one of her assigned chores. "The sink was right under the window, which I believe faced north, and I saw a dark purple bank of stormy-looking clouds with a reddish haze near the bottom. Suddenly I saw a long, black funnel drop out of the clouds and, not knowing what it was at the time, pointed it out to the Sisters. Of course, they immediately took me to the girls' dorm and told me to stay under the bed until they came back for me."

Virginia remembers that a new barn had been added to the convent property not long before the day of the storm. "We had four cows that furnished our milk and butter. I had to churn the milk to make butter, and my reward for completing this job was a big glass of buttermilk. I remember that the new barn was either destroyed or badly damaged, but an old, rickety hen house next to the barn wasn't

Aftermath of the June 1938 tornado, a fallen windmill against the main academy building. *Georgeann Walton.*

hurt a bit. A huge, huge tree that had been there since the late 1800s was uprooted like a matchstick."

While it is commonly thought that the devasting tornado caused the closing of the academy on June 11, 1938, the Order had earlier decided to close the school. The graduating exercises on May 30, 1938, would be the school's last. The academy could not overcome the dire financial circumstances of the Depression years. At the closing exercises, nine junior high school graduates received their diplomas "amid the festive circumstances usually accompanying such occasions." Vacation had begun. Eight sisters and one boarder were in the buildings when the fury of a West Texas tornado emphatically brought an unmistakable end to the institute of Our Lady of Mercy Academy and Convent.

The bishop of the Amarillo Diocese wrote in a tribute to the Stanton Sisters of Mercy who maintained the academy and convent for 44 years: "The Academy of the Sisters of Mercy at Stanton represented a real successful pioneering enterprise which flourished under many difficulties through the generous spirit of devotion to Christian education on the part of the Sisters. The spiritual influence they have exerted cannot be a matter of complete record for so many of their good deeds have no other registry but in the Book of Life."

Chapter 12
An Enduring Heritage

Many stories have been written about the monastery and its history. Often, when the building was deserted, the emphasis was on the tumbleweeds stacked against the gate, the boards covering the windows, and the thick dust and cobwebs inside. Some recounted tales of ghosts haunting the second floor. During those many desolate years, it may have been difficult to recall the strength of mind and spirit that once filled this religious center. And, it was just as challenging to imagine the many children, laughing and learning within those thick adobe walls, who later took the precepts of the academy into the world.

Sister Irma Multer, a student from 1927 to 1930, recalled how the nuns and students helped feed the hungry during the Depression years. This humanitarian service was perhaps beyond the intended scope of the academy and convent, but not beyond the capacity to care by the Sisters. Across these many years, their example continues to serve as a model.

"The late 1920s and early 1930s were years of the Great Depression. Although times were hard, we were always well fed. A typical breakfast consisted of stewed apples, cream of wheat or oatmeal, bread and butter and hot cocoa and coffee au lait for the older students. Sunday brought a special treat of scrambled eggs. At dinner we usually enjoyed beef stew with potatoes and some vegetable, or hominy grits with stewed tomatoes and wieners or egg and cheese souffle and bread; an apple for dessert and hot tea laced with milk. The supper menu was simple. We dined on soup, bread and butter, a glass of milk and ginger-bread or rice pudding for dessert.

"As I pointed out earlier, these were the depression years. I can still see in my mind's eye the long line of hungry men and women standing at the door of the academy waiting for food. We students were asked to hurry through our meals so that the poor could be brought in and fed. The Sisters prepared soup, baked beans and bread to feed the poor. Another girl and I often helped Sister to serve these guests.

"I cherish fond memories of my boarding school days. Especially dear to my heart are memories of the Sisters of Mercy – those ladies of great dignity and refinement. Their devotion and dedication to their profession of educating the young and serving the sick and poor has been a source of inspiration to me throughout my life."

Sister Jan Hayes wrote about a gathering of ten Sisters of Mercy in Stanton in 1995 to observe the 100th Anniversary of the arrival of the Order in West Texas. She remarked that those attending "heard the Mercy spirit in the West Texas wind…" Indeed, the prevailing winds of Martin County can be an ever-present reminder of the richness of the heritage left to us by the dedicated men and women who served at the Monastery of the Most Pure Heart of Mary and Our Lady of Mercy Academy and Convent.

Martin County Convent Foundation

Surviving building of Our Lady of Mercy Academy and Convent during a period of neglect and deterioration. *Martin County Convent Foundation, Inc..*

Window of existing building of Our Lady of Mercy Academy and Convent in 1999 before restoration. *University of North Texas Libraries, The Portal to Texas History, https://texashistory.unt.edu; crediting Texas Historical Commission.*

Exterior door of existing OLM Academy and Convent building in 1999 before restoration. *University of North Texas Libraries, The Portal to Texas History, https://texashistory.unt.edu; crediting Texas Historical Commission.*

Appendix I

Sisters of Mercy
Our Lady of Mercy Academy and Convent
(Partial List)

Name	Birth/Death	Years at Stanton	Responsibilities/Events of Note
Kast, Sr. Mary Berchmans	1844-1939	1894-1938	Founder and Superior of Convent 1894-1913; Chapel duties
Hoestetter, Sr. Mary Angela	1869-1945	1895-21	Head Mistress; taught music; Superior of the Convent 1913-1921; left to join the Foundation in Raton, NM
Reikowsky, Sr. Mary Magdalen	1877-1905	1896-1905	One of 5 sisters buried in St. Joseph Cemetery, Stanton.
Wales, Sr. Mary Vincentia	1868-1928	1898-21	Left to join the Foundation in Raton, NM
Ososky, Sr. Mary Camilla	1878-1952	1899-1921	Left to join the Foundation in Raton, NM
Wernet, Sr. Mary Elizabeth	1852-	1899-1921	Taught music and voice; Mistress of Novices; left to join the Foundation in Raton, NM

Name	Life	Service	Notes
McHugh, Sr. Mary Patricia	1880-1934	1906-1933	Domestic duties; taught grades 4 and 5; one of 5 sisters buried in St. Joseph Cemetery, Stanton
McCabe, Sr. Mary Agnes	1892-1980	1911-1938	Studied pharmacy/Xray in Fort Worth, TX 1928-29; taught grammar school grades
Gasca, Sr. Mary Teresa	1881-1956	1912-30	Teaching, domestic duties, general works, and nursing.
Broderick, Sr. Mary Magdalen	1880-1924	1912-24	One of 5 sisters buried in St. Joseph Cemetery, Stanton.
Fleming, Sr. Mary Cecilia	1893-	1912-29	Came to Stanton from Ireland; taught grades 4 and 6; general duties; withdrew in 1959
Healy, Sr. Mary Augustine	1895-1947	1912-22	Teaching; left to join the Foundation in Raton, NM
Lyons, Sr. Mary Brigid	1892-	1912-31	Came to Stanton from Ireland
Price, Sr. Mary Ignatius	1891-1974	1912-22	Domestic duties
Price, Sr. Mary Xavier	1892-1986	1912-25	Mistress of Novices
Reynolds, Sr. Mary Antonia	1896-1918	1912-18	Came to Stanton from Ireland; withdrew
Salmon, Sr. Mary Columba	1886-1077	1912-34	Domestic; care of children; Mistress of Novices; Reverend Mother; Local Superior of Convent 1929-34
Walsh, Sr. Mary Joseph	1889-1975	1912-37	Supervised boarders at the Academy; Sacristan
Dillon, Sr. Mary Imelda	1884 - 1948	1913-22	General duties; left to join the Foundation in Raton, NM

Martin County Convent Foundation

Nichols, Sr. Mary Francis	1880-1962	1913-30	Domestic duties
Broderick, Sr. Mary Stanislaus	1860-1939	1913-38	Taught elementary grades and music; Superior of Convent (1920-28); Mistress of Novices
Deering, Sr. Mary Gertrude	Unknown - 1917	1913-17	Transferred from Suppressed Convent, Lockhart, TX.; lay Sister at Stanton, domestic duties; one of 5 sisters buried in St. Joseph Cemetery, Stanton.
Hancock, Sr. Mary Monica	1895-	1914-18	Withdrew
DuBronz, Sr. Mary Aloysius	1892-1974	1915-38	Taught high school grades; Superior of the Convent 1934-38
Ellis, Sr. Mary Dolores	1894-1965	1915-21	Withdrew from Stanton in 1921; re-entered at the Foundation in Raton, NM in 1922
Samass Sr. Mary Carmel	1892-	1915-21	Withdrew
Kast, Sr. Mary Mercedes	1866-1949	1916-1921	Came to Stanton at 50 years of age; niece of Sr. Berchmans Kast; left to establish a Foundation in Pecos, NM
Price, Sr. Mary Ignatius		1916	
Garvin, Sr. Margaret Mary	1866-1932	1918-32	One of 5 sisters buried in St. Joseph Cemetery, Stanton
Boney, Sr. Mary Raymond	1892-1963	1919-22	Teacher; to join the Foundation in Raton, NM

Finn, Sr. Mary Consilii	1872-1974	1919-30	Came to the U.S. from Ireland in 1904 at the age of 32;
L'Estrange, Sr. Mary Evangelist	1888-1953	1919-23	Infirmarian; supervised boarders at the Academy; Mistress of Novices
Lynch, Sr. Mary Bernard	1887-	1920-25	Dismissed
Rascon, Sr. Mary Rita	1905-1989	1921-38	Domestic duties; culinary department
Bourgeois, Sr. Mary Josephine	1886-1971	1921-38	Taught primary grades and in charge of boys dormitory
Lundy, Sr. Mary Dympna	1901-1981	1921-28	Came to Stanton from Ireland; taught primary grades
Collazo, Sr. Mary de Cristo	1894-1963	1922-36	Taught primary grades
Barron, Sr. Mary Lourdes	1905-1970	1922-38	Taught primary grades and music
Aycock, Sr. Mary Michael	1906-	1922-29	General duties; taught Latin and supervised boys dormitory (1930)
Molina, Sr. Mary Paula	1902-	1922-25	Withdrew
Jeffries, Sr. Mary Mercedes	1907-1991	1928-29	Transferred to Slaton, Texas where she served over 50 years at Mercy Hospital.
Sparks, Sr. Mary Regina	1910-1976	1928-29	Transferred to Missouri

Appendix II

Articles of Corporation Sisters of Mercy Educational Society of Texas April 23, 1897

This is to certify that this day and date the undersigned have associated themselves together to form a Corporation by the name and for the purpose hereinafter named, to-wit:

1. The name of this Corporation, is, and shall be Sisters of Mercy Educational Society of Texas.
2. The Corporation is formed for the support and protection of school, education, charity, and benevolence, that is to teach in schools, build schools, academies, and hospitals as the wants and necessities of society and humanity may from time to time require, and the means of this Corporation allow and permit.
3. The business of said Corporation shall be transacted at Stanton, Martin County, Texas, in such manner as the by-laws of this Corporation shall prescribe.
4. This corporation shall continue to exist for fifty years.
5. The number of trustees of this Corporation shall be three persons, and the name and residences of the trustees for the first year are

as follows, to-wit: Mother M. Berchmans Kast, Sister M. Angela Hoestetter, Sister M. Magdalen Reikowsky, Stanton, Texas.

This document was filed in the county clerk's office of Martin County, Paul Konz, County Clerk, July 10, 1897. It was filed in the Department of State at Austin, July 12, 1897, and signed by J. W, Madden, Secretary of State.

Appendix III

Sisters of Mercy Educational Society of Texas By-Laws
Filed November 16, 1906
Recorded in Martin County Miscellaneous Record 1, Pages 186-187

The by-laws of the Corporation were as follows:

1. The Mother is <u>ipso</u> <u>facto</u> President of the Corporation.
2. The society and trustees with the president shall constitute the Board of Directors, and shall be elected every two years; if any vacancy appears by death, resignation or otherwise, the remaining directors shall fill the vacancy as soon as possible, appointing a competent member from the society.
3. The society shall consist of all the sisters of Mercy belonging to the Sisters of Mercy Order, at Stanton, who have made the vows of the order according to the rules of the Sisters of Mercy; but only those Sisters who have made professions two years since shall have right to vote, and to be elected into the Board of Directors.
4. To transact important business three directors must be present. The president at all meetings when she is present has the power to receive and transfer property of the Society, to make contracts, to sue and be sued, to appoint agents when necessary, and such

appointments shall be made in writing and attended by her signature, the stamp or seal of the Society.
5. The assistant mother shall have the same power as the president at any meeting if the president is not present; in case of vacancy in the office of president, the mother assistant shall have the power to sign deeds, contracts, etc.

Signed by Sister M. Berchmans, President; Sister M. Angela, Sister M. Magdalen.

Sister M. Magdalen died June 3, 1906. Sister M. Elizabeth has been duly appointed to fill the vacancy, June 6, 1906.

Acknowledgments

Many thanks to the following for their support and contribution to this book:

Carmelite historian Father John-Benedict Weber, O.Carm.
Killis Almond, Historic Architect, San Antonio, Texas
John Kennady, historian and member of the Martin County Convent Foundation
The Archives of Mercy Heritage Center, Sisters of Mercy of the Americas
Martin County Historical Museum
Kathleen Beach
Laura Townes Greene Velez
The Martin County Convent Foundation 2021 Board of Directors: Reggie Baker, Michael Landoll, Thressa Baker, McKenzie Allred, Kim Baker, Lester Baker, Ronda Ireton, Albert H. Baker, Michael Rodriquez, Jackie Smith, Georgeann Walton, Pam Baker, Minerva Garza, John Kennady

Selected Bibliography

Abbe, Don. *Carmelites, Germans, and Marienfeld, Texas*. Panhandle-Plains Historical Review, Panhandle Plains Historical Society, 1983.

Hutto, John. *The German and Catholic Colony of Marienfeld*. West Texas Historical Association Year Book, Vol. 9, 1933.

Jordan, Terry. *German Seed in Texas Soil: Immigrant Farmers in Nineteenth Century Texas*. University of Texas Press, 1966.

Moore, Franchelle. *A History of the Convent and Academy of Our Lady of Mercy, Stanton, Texas*. Permian Historical Annual, Vol. 111, 1963.

O'Brien, R.S.M., Kathleen. *Journeys: a Pre-Amalgamation History of the Sisters of Mercy*. Omaha Province, Sisters of Mercy, 1987.

Schmidt, Ernestine Peters. *Der Peters Familie*. The Gregath Company, 1988.

Weber, O.Carm., John-Benedict. *The Carmelites of Marienfeld*. Journal of Texas Catholic History and Culture, Texas Catholic History Society, Vol. 6, 1995.

About the Author

Rosa Walston Latimer is the author of six historical non-fiction books, a playwright and an award-winning photographer. She has written for national and regional magazines and newspapers and was news editor of a print and an online newspaper and supervising director of a nationally syndicated television program. Rosa was the Flower Hill Urban Homestead Museum, Austin, Texas Writer-in-Residence, 2020-2021.

The story of her Harvey Girl grandmother sparked her interest in preserving women's history and inspired her to write her first book, *Harvey Houses of Texas: Historic Hospitality from the Gulf Coast to the Panhandle* followed by *Harvey Houses of New Mexico*, *Harvey Houses of Kansas*, and *Harvey Houses of Arizona* – all published by The History Press. *Harvey Houses of Kansas* received a 2016 "Notable Kansas Book" award and *Harvey Houses of Texas* was nominated for a Texas Christian University Texas Book Award. Rosa lives in Austin, Texas. **RosaLatimer.org**

Index

A
Abbe, Don 12, 53
Atchison, Vergie Mae (Henson) 83

B
Barron, Sr., Mary Lourdes 99, 100, 101, 112
Brandt, Margaret (Lupton) 84
Broderick, Sister Magdalen 60, 63, 110, 116
Broderick, Sister Stanislaus 54, 60, 72, 96-98, 100, 101, 111

C
Catholic Diocese of Amarillo 98, 104
Cauble, George Clinton 84
Childers, Valdeva Nell 100
Coulter, William A. 61
Curry, Mabel (Sherman) 84

D
Der Peters Familie 14, 25
DuBronz, Sister Aloysius 71, 80, 91
Dunn, Helen 80

E
Esser, Lawrence 48, 49

F
Fahrenkempt, Mrs. W.F. 7
FitzSimon, D.D., Bishop Laurence J. 51, 55, 56, 59
Fuhrwerk, Rev. Andrew 16, 49, 50

G
Glascock, Charles Walker 79
Grelton, Texas 11, 13, 16, 20, 22

H
Hardt, O.Carm., Father Telesphorus 23, 40
Hoestetter, Sister Angela 54, 58, 59, 61, 73, 83, 95, 96, 109, 104, 116
Hutto, John 20, 32

J
Jeffries, Sister Ruth Mercedes 87, 112
Jenkins, Dorothy 90, 92, 94
Jordan, Terry 11

K
Kast, Sister Mary Berchmans 8, 54-59, 95, 96, 109, 114, 116
Keber, Father Anthony 16
Kennady, John 3, 6, 117
Konz, Adam 16, 49, 50
Konz, John Jacob 13

L
Lane, O.P., Sister Claude 52
Lewis, Jack H. 89
Lourdes, Sister Mary 99, 100
Love, 'Light Horse Harry' 42

M
Marienfeld, Estacado and West Texas Steam Transportation 31
Marienfeld Fruit Growing, Gardening and Irrigation 42, 43
Marienfeld, Texas 22-46, 50-53, 55, 56
Martin County 14, 20, 24, 26, 28, 29, 30, 32, 34, 36, 42, 43, 44, 48, 53, 54, 59, 60, 82, 113, 114, 115
Mary's Field *Also See Marienfeld* 5, 6, 22

McAnalley, Bill H. 89
McCabe, Sr. Mary Agnes 67, 101, 110
McGinnis, Jim 89
McHenry, Paul G. 2, 33
Monastery of the Most Pure Heart of Mary 8, 15, 17, 20, 34, 35, 36, 39, 44, 47, 48
Multer, Sister Irma 68, 69, 70, 105
Mundloch, Nicholas 24, 25

N

Neraz, Bishop John C. 17, 20, 44, 57

O

O'Brien, R.S.M., Kathleen 57, 95
Ohlenforst, Father Berthold 16
"Our Lady of Mercy Academy and Convent 2, 8, 55-59, 61, 66, 67, 70, 73, 77, 79, 83, 85, 89, 90, 96, 97, 106, 109"
Owen, Elizabeth (Lupton) 85

P

Peters, Christian Dominikus. *See* Peters, Father Anastasius
Peters, Father Anastasius 13, 14, 15, 17-22, 24-28, 33, 34, 41, 42, 44, 45, 46, 49, 50,
Peters, Father Boniface 14-18, 24, 26, 37, 46
Peters, Father Hubertus 15, 18, 19
Peters, Frederick 24
Peters, Johann Jacob 24, 25, 44
Peters, Christian Leonard. *See* Peters, Father Boniface
Peters, Margaretha. *See* Mundloch 25, 44
Peters, Maria Anna (Straub) 44
Peters, Peter. *See* Peters, Father Hubertus
Peters, Ingatius "Ick" George 44
Phillip, Gustav 27, 28
Pope, Capt. John 11
Price, Sister Xavier 60, 67, 97, 98, 107, 110
Pritchett, Lauryn Westerman 82

R

Rawlins, A. 42
Reikowsky, Sr. Mary Magdalen 59, 64, 109, 114
Ringener, Lena Lynelle (Hasey) 79
Roesler, Frank 42, 46
Rosenthal, Marcelle (Sally) McAnalley 89
Rules of Daily Living 34

S

Salmon, Sr. Mary Columba 54, 60, 71, 73, 110
San Antonio Diocese 17, 44
Sanchez, Nick 90
Schulze, Blythe Weaver 62
Schwarzenbach, Delia Cecilia (Scholz) 77
Scott, Alvin 80, 81, 82
Scott, Dollie 80, 81
Scott, Nannie (Smythe) 80
Sirius, O.M.I., Father J.O. 48, 50
Sisters of Divine Providence 7, 51, 52, 53
Sisters of Mercy 54, 55, 59, 63, 70, 73, 74, 82, 84, 109
Smet, O. C., Father Joachim 20
Smits, Father 16, 17, 18, 19, 20
Smythe, Peter 82
Staked Plains of Texas 11, 20, 26, 42
Stanton, Texas 1, 33, 43, 46, 55, 74, 104, 113
St. Boniface Monastery 15, 16
St. Joseph Cemetery 25, 64, 82, 110, 111
St. Joseph Church 22, 33

T

Texas and Pacific Railway 7, 11, 13, 22, 24, 37, 38, 42
Tom, Sister Angela 90, 91, 92, 94

U

Urey, Virginia (Ragland) 103

W

Walton, Georgeann 8, 13, 14, 24, 28, 67, 68, 117
Wagner O.Carm., Father Albert 16, 17, 44, 45
Weber, O.Carm., John-Benedict 16, 32, 37, 45, 48, 119
Weeg, O.Carm., Father Simon 17, 36, 38, 57
White, Sophie (Jeffries) 87
World's Industrial and Cotton Centennial Exposition 28

Y

York, Emmagene (Davis) 86

Thanks to the tireless effort of many volunteers, community leaders, and generous donors, the 1884 monastery stands today as a fully restored historic landmark in Martin County. This magnificent structure features a rare blend of Mexican adobe and German Gothic architecture. A walk inside the building takes you back to re-live rustic monastic life on the West Texas frontier. Please visit our website for more information and a calendar of events. Photo by Conrad Coleman.

Martin County Convent Foundation
P.O. Box 1435
Stanton, Texas 79782
hcmstanton.org
historiccarmelitemonastery@gmail.com
Follow us on Facebook at Martin County Convent

Contact us for a tour of the restored property of
Our Lady of Mercy Academy and Convent or for information
about scheduling a special event or photo opportunity.

www.ingramcontent.com/pod-product-compliance
Lightning Source LLC
Chambersburg PA
CBHW022018290426
44109CB00015B/1224